THE EXPLORER'S BIBLE

Volume 2: From Sinai to the Nation of Israel

BY SCOTT E. BLUMENTHAL

Behrman House Publishers
www.behrmanhouse.com

PROJECT MANAGER:	Gila Gevirtz
BOOK AND COVER DESIGN:	Howard Levy/Red Rooster Group
STORY ILLUSTRATION:	Risa Towbin Aqua
ACTIVITY ILLUSTRATION:	Stuart Harrison
ICON ILLUSTRATION:	Jim Steck
EDITORIAL COMMITTEE:	Martin S. Cohen, Dina Maiben,
	Ellen J. Rank, Sunny Yudkoff

The publisher and author gratefully acknowledge the following sources of photographs and graphic images: **Atlantide Phototravel/Corbis** 108–109; **David E. Behrman** 12, 28, 78, 88, 120; **Bildarchiv Preussischer Kulturbesitz/Art Resources, NY** 50; **John Conrad/Corbis** 68; **Creative Image** 20, 60; **Gustav Doré** 24; **Gila Gevirtz** 138; **Grace/zefa/Corbis** 146; **The Jewish Museum, NY/Art Resources, NY** 41; **Mark A. Johnson/Corbis** 154; **Steve Kaufman/Corbis** 8; **Terry Kaye** 52, 96; **Richard Klune/Corbis** 112; **Bruce Laurance/Getty Images** cover; **Erich Lessing/Art Resources, NY** 73, 95, 116–118, 126, 134, 150; **Richard Lobell** 36; **Gideon Mendel/Corbis** 57; **Richard T. Nowitz/Corbis** 65, 82–83; **Jose Luis Pelaez/zefa/Corbis** 44; **Jeremy Poisson** 128; **Réunion des Musées Nationaux/Art Resources, NY** 100; **Ricki Rosen/Corbis** 33; **Spc Katherine M. Roth/HO/epa/Corbis** 142–143; **Templer/zefa/Corbis** 104

To Eve, our first

Contents

CHAPTER 1

The Great Miracle

EXODUS 13:17–15:35

ויבקעו המים

EXODUS 13:17–22

After many generations of slavery in Egypt, the Israelites were finally free. Now, God led the people to the Promised Land, the land of Canaan. God led them away from the land of the Philistines, even though it was near. Instead, God led them through the desert, by way of the Sea of Reeds. God guided the Israelites in a pillar of cloud by day and a pillar of fire by night.

The Philistines were among the most feared enemies of the Israelites.

EXODUS 14:1–9

As the Israelites approached the Sea of Reeds, God said to Moses, "I will harden Pharaoh's heart, and he will chase after them. Then I will defeat Pharaoh and his army. This way, the Egyptians will know that I am God." When Pharaoh heard that the Israelites had gone, he said, "Why did we let the Israelites go? They are our slaves!" He gathered an army with six hundred chariots and chased after the Israelites.

Looking at this picture of the Sinai Desert, what difficulties and fears do you think our ancestors might have experienced? What might have given them the courage to keep moving forward?

Think of a time in your life when you accomplished something important, even though you were afraid.

EXODUS 14:10–14

The Israelites saw the Egyptian army coming toward them and became afraid. They said to Moses, "Did you bring us here to die? It would have been better for us to remain slaves than to die here in the desert!" Moses said to the people, "Do not be afraid. God will rescue you. The Egyptians you see today you will never see again!"

The Long Way Home

כִּי קָרוֹב הוּא

God did not lead the Israelites to the land of the Philistines *ki karov hu*, "even though it was near." But why take the long way on purpose? Our sages give us these suggestions:

- **Rashi teaches:** The word *ki* means "even though," but also "because." God wanted the Israelites to avoid the Philistines *because* they might become afraid and turn back.

- **The Talmud teaches:** The word *karov* means "near," but also "special." God did not lead the Israelites into danger because they are *special* to God.

- **Ibn Ezra teaches:** God wanted the Israelites to have time to experience freedom— and to learn how to live as free people—before settling in their new home.

EXODUS 14:15–22

Then God said to Moses, "Lift up the rod in your hand and hold it high. The sea will split, so that the Israelites may march through on dry ground." Moses did as God had commanded. God lashed at the sea with a powerful wind. The waters split, and the Israelites went through on dry ground. The waters were huge walls to the left and the right of the Israelites.

People sometimes call this famous sea the Red Sea, but it wasn't. The Red Sea was probably more than a hundred miles away.

Exodus 14:23–31

Pharaoh's soldiers chased after the Israelites, but God locked the wheels of their chariots so that they could barely move. The soldiers said, "Let us flee from the Israelites. God is fighting for them against Egypt!" Then God said to Moses, "Hold out your arm over the sea, and the walls of water will fall upon the Egyptians." Moses held out his arm, and the sea covered Pharaoh's army. Not one Egyptian soldier survived. This is how God saved Israel from the Egyptians.

Walls of Water

Flashback! Imagine that you are walking on dry land through the Sea of Reeds. Write a description of how you feel or draw a picture of what you see.

Exodus 15:1–18

Moses and the Israelites sang a song to God:
> Who is like You, among the gods, Adonai?
> Who is like You, majestic in holiness,
> Awesome in greatness, doing wonders!

We recall these words from the "Song of the Sea" during prayer services, when we sing Mi Chamocha, "Who is like You?"

Exodus 15:20–22

Miriam the prophet, the sister of Aaron and Moses, took a timbrel in her hand, and all the women danced with her. Then Moses led the Israelites from the Sea of Reeds into the desert, toward Canaan.

A *timbrel* is a small hand drum, similar to today's tambourine.

Exodus 15:23–16:35

When the people became thirsty, God provided water. When the people became hungry, God sent a fine, flaky substance that covered the ground like frost. The people discovered that it tasted like wafers dipped in honey. They called it manna. Every day, for five days, the people gathered one portion of manna. On the sixth day, they gathered a double portion—an additional portion for the seventh day, Shabbat, the day of rest. The Israelites would eat manna every day for the next forty years.

The Faith of One

Our sages told this story: When Moses first held his hand over the sea, nothing happened. He ordered the Israelites to move forward, but they were too afraid. Suddenly, Naḥshon, son of Aminadav, stepped forward and dipped a toe into the sea. At first, nothing happened. Naḥshon continued walking until the water was to his waist. Nothing. To his chin. Still nothing. Finally, just as the water reached Naḥshon's lips, the sea burst open and the Israelites walked to safety. All along, God had been waiting for a sign of faith.

Sometimes we must make choices based only on what we *feel* or *believe*. Like Naḥshon at the Sea of Reeds, we place one foot ahead of the other and go. We put our faith in God—and in ourselves.

What is the difference between a leap of faith and a risky action or behavior?

Leapin' Lizards!

To make good decisions, you often need to gather *information*

learn from *experience* and use *good judgment*

But sometimes you also need to take a *leap of faith*

For each item below, put a check (✔) in as many columns as you would need in order to make a good decision.				
1. How much time to study for a test.				
2. Which summer camp to attend.				
3. Whether or not to smoke cigarettes.				
4. When to go to sleep on a school night.				
5. Who to confide in.				
6. Who to choose as a study partner.				
7. What movie to see.				
8. Which pet to buy.				
9. Where to hide the afikomen on Passover.				
10. When to tell a parent that you lost your library book.				

CHAPTER 2

God's Gift

Exodus 19:1–34:32

וִיתְרוֹ קָבַּלַת
וּבְרָכִים

Exodus 19:1–6

On the third moon after the Israelites left Egypt, they arrived at a mountain in the desert of Sinai. God called Moses to the top of the mountain and said to him, "Remind the people that I brought them out of slavery on eagles' wings. Tell them that if they obey My commands, they will be My treasured people and a holy nation."

Think of a time when you reached a special moment in your life. Why was it special? How did you feel at the time?

Exodus 19:10–14

God continued, "Tell the people to get ready, for in three days I will appear on Mount Sinai. Warn them: Do not touch the mountain. Wash your bodies and your clothing. Only when you hear the blast of a ram's horn may you approach the mountain." Moses came down the mountain and delivered God's instructions to the people.

Why do you think that God wanted the people to wash themselves before approaching the mountain?

This modern wall hanging by Naomi Hordes reminds us of the biblical teaching that God brought the Israelites out of slavery on eagles' wings. What do you think this teaching means?

EXODUS 19:16–20:1

On the third day, as the sun came up, thunder, lightning, and a heavy cloud covered the mountain. There was a loud blast of the ram's horn. The blast grew louder and louder. The people trembled. Mount Sinai, covered in smoke, trembled violently. God came down upon Mount Sinai and spoke these words to the people:

EXODUS 20:2–14

1. I am Adonai your God who brought you out of the land of Egypt.
2. Have no other gods before Me. Do not worship an image of anything that is in heaven or on earth.
3. Do not use My name for dishonest purposes.
4. Remember Shabbat and keep it holy. Six days you will work, but on the seventh day you will rest.
5. Honor your father and your mother.
6. Do not murder.
7. Do not be unfaithful to your wife or husband.
8. Do not steal.
9. Do not falsely accuse a neighbor.
10. Do not wish to possess anything that belongs to your neighbor.

The tenth commandment is the only one to forbid a feeling, not an action. In your opinion, why was this commandment included?

Exodus 21:1–24:7

Later, God gave more laws to the people, including:

🍃 When you find something that has been lost, you must return it to its owner.

🍃 Do not mistreat a stranger, for you were strangers in Egypt.

🍃 For six years you will gather the harvest from your fields. During the seventh year, let the needy among you gather the harvest for themselves.

When the people heard these laws, they answered with one voice, "All that God has commanded we will do and we will obey!"

yes We Will!

נַעֲשֶׂה וְנִשְׁמָע

At the heart of the prayer service, we proclaim, as a community, our declaration of faith: *Sh'ma, Yisrael!* Usually, we translate these words as, "Hear, O Israel!" But like many Hebrew words, *sh'ma* has several meanings.

Sh'ma means "hear," but also "obey," "listen," and "understand." After Moses reads the laws to the Children of Israel, the people respond, *na'aseh v'nishma*, "we will do and we will obey." Or hear or listen or understand. With this important word, the Israelites show they are ready and willing to receive and follow God's laws.

In ancient times, bulls and calves were symbols of leadership and strength.

EXODUS 24:12–18; 32:1–6

After that, God called Moses to the top of the mountain. Moses said to the people, "Wait here until I return." Moses remained on the mountain forty days and forty nights. On the fortieth day, the people said to Aaron, "We do not know what happened to Moses. Make us an idol to lead us." Aaron said to the people, "Gather your gold and bring it to me." Aaron took the gold and formed it into a golden calf. The people made sacrifices and worshiped the idol.

EXODUS 32:15–20

Moses came down from the mountain carrying two tablets of stone, on which the Ten Commandments were written. When Moses saw the people dancing around the golden calf, he burned with anger. He threw down the tablets, shattering them at the foot of the mountain. To punish the people, he ground the calf into powder, mixed it with water, and made the Israelites drink it.

EXODUS 34:1–4, 28–32

God said to Moses, "Carve two new tablets of stone, and I will write on them the same words as the first." Moses did as God had commanded and went up Mount Sinai. He was on the mountain for another forty days and forty nights. When he came down, his face was glowing because he had spoken with God. Moses called the Israelites near and taught them everything that God had told him.

The Righteous Women

MIDRASH MAKER

Question

Why did Aaron make the golden calf? Didn't he know better than to create an idol?

Classic Midrash

Aaron did not want to create the golden calf, but he wanted to calm the people. So he thought of a plan: He told the men to ask their *wives* for their gold jewelry. He thought, "The women are righteous. They will refuse to give up their gold for such a terrible purpose. Then the whole matter will come to nothing."

But Aaron was only partly successful. The women *did* refuse to give up their gold for an idol that could help no one. The men, however, gave their *own* gold to Aaron. Aaron's plan to prevent the creation of the golden calf did not work. (adapted from Pirkei de Rabbi Eliezer 45)

Your Midrash

Imagine that you are Aaron. The people are growing worried that Moses will not return from Mount Sinai. They ask you to "make a god" to lead them. Think of three reasons you might give them to help them change their minds.

1. _____

_____

2. _____

_____

3. _____

_____

Holy, Holy, Holy!

In Hebrew, the word meaning "holy" is related to the word meaning "set apart." When we make something holy, we set it apart from other things.

Holiness is everywhere in this chapter:

- If the Israelites follow God's commands, God will make them a *holy nation*. They will be set apart from other nations.
- Only Moses can go up Mount Sinai *for it is holy*. It is set apart from other places.
- The fourth commandment tells us to make Shabbat *holy*. It will be set apart from the other days.
- By teaching us to set things apart, the Bible reminds us of the holiness that is all around us.

The Jewish year has many special days that are holy. Which holy day do we celebrate every week? What other holy days can you name?

A Picture of Holiness

While many things may be special, for example, birthday cakes, vacations, and rainbows, Judaism teaches that holiness is more than just being special—holiness connects us to godliness and guides us to the path of compassion, peace, and justice. We find holiness in the peace and beauty of Shabbat, in acts of loving-kindness, in all the creatures of God's world, and in every mitzvah we perform.

In the space below, draw a scene that is filled with images of the holiness in your life. For example, you may want to include family members and friends, your favorite Jewish holiday, or yourself performing a mitzvah.

CHAPTER 3

The Courage of Two

NUMBERS 13:1–20:12; DEUTERONOMY 31:1–34:12

זבת חלב ודבש

NUMBERS 13:1–20

God said to Moses, "I will now lead the Israelites into the land of Canaan, the land that I promised to Abraham, Isaac, and Jacob. Select twelve men, one from each tribe, to scout out the land."

Moses did as God had commanded. He said to the scouts, "Go and see what kind of land it is. Are its people strong or weak? Are there many of them? Are their towns well protected?" And Moses sent the scouts into Canaan.

The Israelites were divided into twelve tribes, each named for one of Jacob's sons. Each tribe would later establish its own region in the land of Canaan.

NUMBERS 13:25–33

After forty days, the scouts returned. They brought with them a cluster of grapes so large that two men were needed to carry it. Ten of the scouts announced to Moses and the Israelites, "The land flows with milk and honey, and this is its fruit. However, the people there are powerful, and their cities are well protected." But the other two scouts, Joshua and Caleb, said to the people, "God will bring us into the land. Have no fear!" The ten scouts replied, "No—if we enter the land, we will be defeated. The people we saw looked like giants. We must have looked like grasshoppers to them!"

Think of a time when you saw only the negative side of a situation. Why do you think you did that?

The scouts described the Promised Land as "flowing with milk and honey." What is the most wonderful place that you have ever been to? How would you describe it?

Why do you think the community became angry with Joshua and Caleb?

NUMBERS 14:1–19

The Israelites grew afraid and said, "Why is God taking us to that land to die? Let us go back to Egypt!" They became angry with Joshua and Caleb and threatened to throw stones at them. God said to Moses, "How long will this people have no faith in Me? I will not bring them into the land." But Moses said, "Please, forgive these people."

Numbers 14:20–35

God said, "I will not forgive those who saw the miracles I performed in Egypt. I will allow only their children to enter. Tell the people: You will roam the desert for forty years—one year for every day that you scouted the land—until the last of you dies in the desert. But My servants Joshua and Caleb, because they remained loyal to Me, will enter the land." So God made the people wander in the desert until the generation that had worshiped the golden calf died.

Numbers 20:2–12

For forty years, the Israelites wandered through the desert. Then, once again, they complained to Moses. "Why did you make us leave Egypt to bring us to this terrible place, a place with no grain or figs or vines? There is not even water to drink!"

The Bible tells us little about the forty-year journey through the desert. What do you think it was like to wander for so long without a home?

God said to Moses, "Assemble the community, and order the rock to bring forth its water." Moses assembled the people. He raised his hand and struck the rock twice with his rod. Water poured out, and the people and animals drank. Then God said to Moses, "Because you did not do as I commanded you, because you did not trust me, you will not lead this community into the land that I had given them."

Deuteronomy 31:1–8

Later, Moses spoke to the people: "I am now one hundred and twenty years old, and I am tired. I will not enter the land of Canaan. But God will protect you and Joshua will lead you. Do not be afraid." Then Moses said to Joshua, "Be strong and brave, for you will lead the people to the Promised Land."

A Chat with Moses

MIDRASH MAKER

Question

God commanded Moses to speak to the rock. Why did Moses strike the rock instead? And why twice?

Classic Midrash

Even after many years of wandering, the Israelites threatened to return to Egypt. This made Moses furious. Carried away by anger, Moses struck the rock instead of speaking to it, as God had commanded. Because Moses had not obeyed God's command, the rock sent forth only a few drops of water. The Israelites teased Moses, and he grew even more angry. So he struck the rock a second time. This time, it gushed mighty streams of water. (based on Yalkut Shimoni, Numbers, Chapter 20)

Your Midrash

Imagine that you are Moses. The Israelites have come to you with the following questions. How will you answer them?

Why did you strike the rock and not speak to it, as God had commanded you?

_____

_____

_____

You are not allowed to enter Canaan. Do you think that your punishment is fair? Why or why not?

_____

_____

_____

Deuteronomy 31:9–13; 34:5–12

Then Moses wrote down the words of the Teaching. He said to the elders of the community, "Gather the people—the men, women, children, and the strangers among you—to hear the Teaching, so that they may learn to respect God." Soon after, Moses died. Never again did there arise a prophet like Moses.

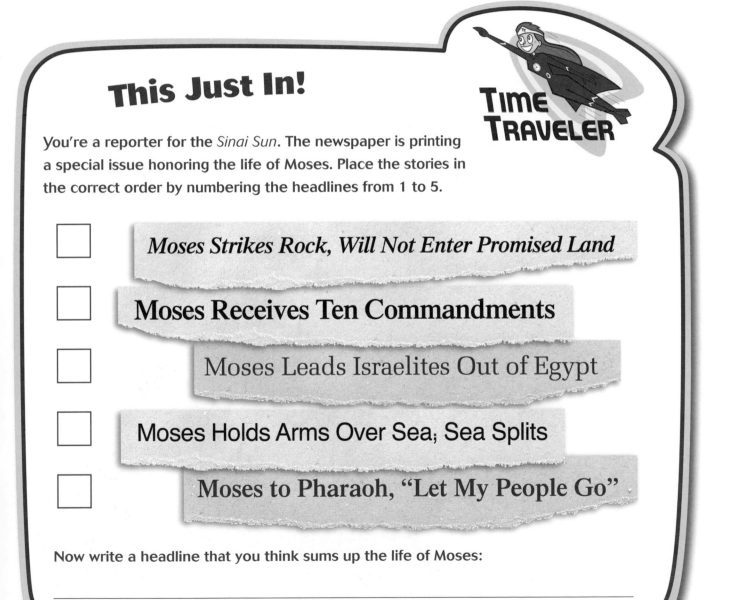

This Just In!

Time Traveler

You're a reporter for the *Sinai Sun*. The newspaper is printing a special issue honoring the life of Moses. Place the stories in the correct order by numbering the headlines from 1 to 5.

☐ *Moses Strikes Rock, Will Not Enter Promised Land*

☐ **Moses Receives Ten Commandments**

☐ Moses Leads Israelites Out of Egypt

☐ Moses Holds Arms Over Sea; Sea Splits

☐ **Moses to Pharaoh, "Let My People Go"**

Now write a headline that you think sums up the life of Moses:

_____

Positive Power

Ten scouts warn the Israelites not to enter the land. It is filled with powerful, dangerous people, they say, who wish them harm. But two scouts, Joshua and Caleb, explain that the Israelites *should* enter the land. The people should not be afraid because God will be with them.

All twelve scouts embarked on an important but dangerous mission. All twelve scouts saw the same land and the same people. But only Joshua and Caleb saw hope and promise. Only they had the courage to disagree with the majority and the optimism to move forward. It was this courage and optimism that inspired the Israelites to enter the land—and to never look back.

If you were asked to name the color of courage, what would it be? What might the color of optimism be?

Captain Courage

Captain Courage builds up her positive attitude and her courage by eating Snizzle Snap Cereal. Sometimes, when faced with a *really* big challenge, she must eat an extra bowl or two. Next to each item below, check the number of bowls of Snizzle Snap you think Captain Courage will need in order to face her fears and to overcome the challenge.

Be prepared to discuss your answers.

	1 bowl	2 bowls	3 bowls	4 bowls	5 bowls
1. Learn to ride a bike.					
2. Admit that she accidentally broke her brother's watch.					
3. Go to a party where she doesn't know *anyone*.					
4. Recite the Four Questions in Hebrew on Passover.					
5. Make a speech.					
6. Tell her parents that she forgot to walk the dog.					
7. Help someone who is being bullied.					

CHAPTER 4

Joshua Fights for Freedom

JOSHUA 1:1–8:35

וַיָּרִעוּ הָעָם תְּרוּעָה גְדוֹלָה

JOSHUA 1:1–9

God said to Joshua, "Prepare to lead the Israelites across the Jordan River, into the land that I promised them. Your territory will stretch from Lebanon in the north, to the desert in the south, to the Euphrates River in the east, to the Mediterranean Sea in the west. Remember to faithfully observe the Teaching that Moses gave to you. Only then will you prosper. Only then will you succeed. Do not be afraid, for I am with you wherever you go."

The Bible is divided into three sections: the Torah, the Prophets, and the Writings. Joshua is the first book of the Prophets.

JOSHUA 2:1

God said to Joshua, "I will deliver the city of Jericho into your hands." So Joshua sent two spies into Jericho to learn its strengths and weaknesses. Once inside the city, the spies came to the house of a woman named Rahab. Rahab hid the spies on the roof of her house.

The city of Jericho—like many ancient cities—was surrounded by high, protective walls of earth and stone.

JOSHUA 2:2–7

The king of Jericho heard that spies had entered the city—and that Rahab was hiding them. He sent soldiers to Rahab's house. The soldiers said to Rahab, "Surrender the men who came to you. They are spies." Rahab said, "It is true that the men were here, but last night, when the city gate was about to be closed, the men left. I do not know where they went. If you go now, you can catch them!" So the soldiers left to pursue the spies.

Agree or disagree: We must sometimes stretch the truth in order to protect someone. Explain your answer.

JOSHUA 2:8–15

Rahab went up to the roof. She said to the men, "We have heard how your God split the waters of the Sea of Reeds when you left Egypt. We know that your God has given the land to you. Everyone in the land is trembling. Now, since I have shown kindness to you, please spare my family when you take this land." The men answered, "If you keep our mission a secret, we will show mercy to you and your family when God gives us the land." Rahab agreed and lowered them by a rope over the city wall.

According to midrash, Rahab and Joshua were later married.

JOSHUA 6:1–5

Jericho closed its gates. No one could leave or enter. God said to Joshua, "Have your troops march in a circle around the city. Do this for six days. On the seventh day, march around the city seven times, carrying the Ark of God's Covenant with you, with the priests blowing their horns all the while. When the priests sound a long blast on the horns, command the people to give a mighty shout. The city walls will collapse, and the people will enter the city."

After receiving the Ten Commandments, the Israelites built the Ark of God's Covenant in which to carry the tablets.

Archaeologists study the remains of earlier cultures, including items such as tools, jewelry, and pottery. These archaeologists are studying the remains of Jericho, helping us learn about the history and lives of our ancestors.

The Name Game

Question

Why doesn't the Bible tell us more about the spies who enter Jericho? We don't even know their names!

Classic Midrash

The Bible does not name the spies. Why? To teach us that the spies did not care about fame or praise. Instead, they were concerned only with the success of their mission. From this we learn that when people conduct themselves with modesty, their missions will be successful. But when the wicked set about to accomplish something, they will fail. (adapted from Tanchuma, Shelach 1)

Your Midrash

Read the Hebrew names below. Choose the two names that you think best describe the spies. For each, give a reason for your choice.

Baruch / blessed
Gavriel / God is my strength
Shimon / to hear
Aryeh / lion of God
Shlomo / peace

Name #1: _____
Reason:
_____
_____

Name #2: _____
Reason:
_____
_____

JOSHUA 6:8–24

So the troops circled the city once every day for six days. On the seventh day, they circled the city seven times. During the seventh time around, as the priests blew their horns, Joshua commanded the people, "Shout, for God has given you the city! Only Rahab and her family are to be spared!" So the people raised a mighty shout, and the walls of Jericho collapsed. The people rushed into the city and captured it. The spies brought Rahab and her family outside the city. The Israelites burned the city of Jericho and everything in it.

JOSHUA 8:1–35

God was with Joshua, who conquered all of the Promised Land. After one battle in which he captured the city of Ai, Joshua built an altar of stones. On it he inscribed the Teaching that Moses had written for the Israelites. He read from the Teaching before the entire assembly of Israel, as well as before the strangers who were with them.

God's Reminder

As we grow older and more mature, we earn more freedom—the freedom to ride our bicycles across the street, to stay up late, and to choose what to eat for breakfast. But with more freedom comes more responsibility. We become responsible for wearing a helmet when riding a bike, responsible for getting enough sleep, and responsible for not eating ten cupcakes on the way to school.

When the Children of Israel reached Canaan, finally able to enjoy their freedom, God tells them to "faithfully observe the Teaching that Moses gave to you." God reminds us that freedom gives us choices. Although it allows us to help others and ourselves, it also permits us to ignore the reason we were given freedom—to serve God. God's reminder helps us to remember the blessings and the responsibilities that come with freedom.

Jewish tradition teaches us to balance the responsibility of taking care of our own needs and wants with the responsibility of sharing with those in need. Giving tzedakah is one way of sharing.

Big Bob's Balancing Act

Big Bob walks the Tightrope of Responsibility with the greatest of ease when his concern for himself is in balance with his concern for others. Help Big Bob walk the tightrope by writing three actions that show he takes care of himself and three actions that show he helps others.

A hint from Big Bob: **The sage Hillel taught, "If I am not for myself, who is? If I am only for myself, what am I? And, if not now, when?" How can this teaching remind you to keep your life in balance?**

CHAPTER 5

Deborah's Help

JOSHUA 23:1-24:29, JUDGES 2:10-5:31

ותהיא יושבת
תחת־תמר
דבורה

JOSHUA 23:1–24:29

The Israelites had lived in the Promised Land for many years. One day, Joshua called the people together and said, "I have grown old, and soon I will die. Always remember to observe what is written in the Teaching of Moses. Do not worship other gods or God will take you from this land." Then Joshua taught the people about their ancestors, about the plagues in Egypt, and about the parting of the Sea of Reeds. He asked the people, "Do you promise to serve God?" The people responded, "Yes! We will serve none but Adonai, our God." Soon after, Joshua died.

Why is it important to learn our family's history? How can it help us to live better lives? How can you learn more about your family's history?

39

Israel's Judges were like today's judges in that they settled disputes and made legal decisions. But they were also warriors who led the people into battle.

JUDGES 2:10–3:31

Meanwhile, other nations grew strong and threatened to destroy Israel. The people cried out to God for help. So God gave them leaders called Judges to protect them from their enemies. Judges such as Ehud, who brought peace to Israel for eighty years, and Shamgar, who defeated the cruel Philistines, were among Israel's first Judges. But there was peace only while each Judge was alive. When a judge died, Israel's enemies would again grow stronger and threaten to destroy it. And again God would give the people another Judge. This went on for many years.

JUDGES 4:1–5

One of Israel's greatest judges was the prophet Deborah. Deborah would sit under a tree called the Palm of Deborah, and the Israelites would come to her for help in making important decisions. While she was judge, the Israelites were defeated by the cruel King Jabin of Canaan and his army commander, Sisera.

When you want help with a tough decision, who do you go to for advice?

JUDGES 4:6–9

Deborah called upon Barak, the commander of her army. She said to him, "Take ten thousand men and march up to Mount Tabor. I will lure Sisera and his army into your hands." But Barak said to Deborah, "I will only go if you go with me. If not, I will not go." Deborah said, "Very well. I will go with you. But know that you will not receive glory when Sisera is defeated by a woman."

The Torah commands us to treat others with fairness and justice, and to care for those in need. How might Deborah's judgments have been influenced by those teachings?

JUDGES 4:14–21

When Sisera's army saw Barak and his ten thousand men, they flew into a panic. Sisera leaped from his chariot and ran away. Barak chased after Sisera's army and defeated it. All of Sisera's soldiers died. But Sisera had fled to the tent of Yael, whose husband was a friend of the Canaanite king. Yael said to Sisera, "Come in; do not be afraid. I will hide you." Once Sisera was inside, she covered him with a blanket. When he was fast asleep from exhaustion, Yael snuck up on him with a tent peg and a hammer. She drove the peg through his head, all the way down to the ground, and Sisera died.

Remember Deborah's prediction that Sisera would be defeated by a woman? As it turns out, she was speaking of another brave woman: Yael.

On that day, Deborah and Barak sang this song:

> Hear, O kings!
> I will sing, will sing to Adonai,
> Will sing praises to Adonai, God of Israel.
>
> Freedom was gone
> Gone from Israel,
> Till you arose, O Deborah,
> Arose, O mother of Israel!

Thanks to Deborah, the land was peaceful for forty years.

A Clean Start

אַרְבָּעִים

The number "forty"—*arba'iym*—has a special place in the Bible. It's a clue that we've reached a time of change, a time for a "clean start":

- After Noah boarded the ark, God wiped out life on earth by sending rain for forty days.
- The Israelites wandered for forty years, until the *creators* of the golden calf had died.
- Later, the prophet Jonah will give the wicked city of Nineveh forty days to change its wicked ways.

After Deborah brings peace to Israel, we begin a new era of peace. For how long? Forty years.

Wanted: Judge

Flashback! **You're on a job interview to become the next judge of Israel. The interviewer asks: In what ways are you like Deborah? In what ways are you different? Compare your qualities to Deborah's, and then complete the interview.**

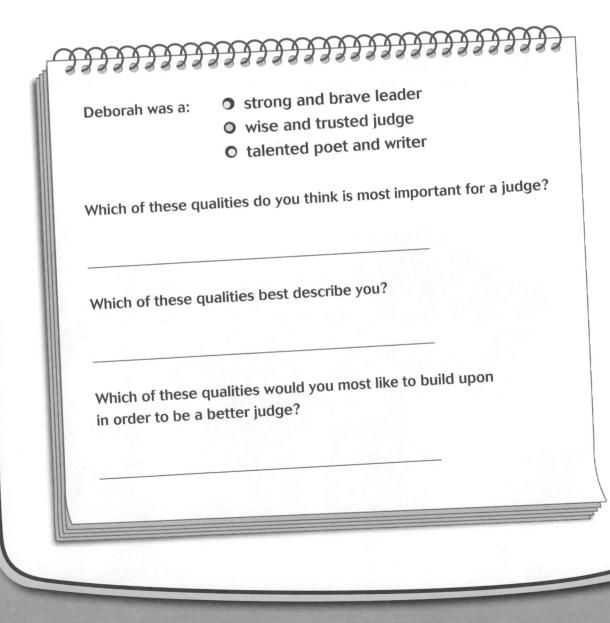

Deborah was a:
- strong and brave leader
- wise and trusted judge
- talented poet and writer

Which of these qualities do you think is most important for a judge?

_____

Which of these qualities best describe you?

_____

Which of these qualities would you most like to build upon in order to be a better judge?

_____

Help!

The story of Deborah is a story of people asking for help: The Israelites ask God for help in their time of need. The people ask Deborah for help when making important decisions. Deborah asks Barak for help in leading the army to victory.

It's not always easy to ask for help. We may feel embarrassed or afraid that the answer may be no. We think that if we ask for help, we're not as strong or smart as we should be. But the opposite is true. Judaism teaches us that it takes courage to ask for help—and that when we do, we strengthen ourselves and our community.

Sometimes the best and the most fun way to accomplish a goal or get a job done is to work with others!

Mount Mega-Mazal

It is said that we make our own *mazal*, or luck. This means that when we work hard to succeed, we are more likely to succeed. There are tasks that are best done with the help of others and those that are best done by ourselves.

In order to climb Mount Mega-Mazal you must accomplish a series of tasks, either by yourself or by getting a helping hand from others. As you follow the trail up the mountain, draw a line to the helping hand in those places where you think it would be most effective to reach out for help.

CHAPTER 6

Samson's Purpose

JUDGES 13:1–16:31

וַיֹּאמֶר שִׁמְשׁוֹן הַמֵּת נַפְשִׁי עִם־פְּלִשְׁתִּים

JUDGES 13:1–25

It was a terrible time for Israel. The Philistines had captured the land and ruled harshly for forty years. One day, an angel of God appeared to a woman from the tribe of Dan. The angel said, "You will have a son. Do not cut his hair, for he will be a Nazirite to God. When he grows up, he will save the Israelites from the Philistines." Soon after, the woman gave birth to a son. She named him Samson. As the boy grew up, the spirit of God stirred in him.

Nazirites dedicated their lives to God and lived by strict rules. They were not allowed to cut their hair, our sages taught, because they were to focus on God—not on their looks!

JUDGES 14:1–15:3

Later, Samson married a Philistine woman. But Samson and his wife did not get along. One day, Samson became angry and stormed out of their home. By the time he returned, his wife was gone. Her father said, "I was sure that you did not like her, so I gave her to another man." Samson said, "Now I have a reason to act against the Philistines. Now I cannot be blamed for the harm I will do them."

What's the closest you've ever come to feeling that you were "gripped by the spirit of God"?

JUDGES 15:4–15

Samson caught three hundred foxes, tied torches to their tails, and sent them into the fields of the Philistines. The fire spread and burned their grain and vineyards. The Israelites said to Samson, "Because you did this, the Philistines will make our lives harder!" They decided to bring Samson to the Philistines and bound him with ropes. But the spirit of God gripped Samson. He snapped the ropes as if they were fibers touching fire. Then Samson took the jawbone of a donkey and used it to kill a thousand Philistines.

JUDGES 16:4–9

Soon after, Samson fell in love with a Philistine woman named Delilah. The leaders of the Philistines said to Delilah, "Find out how we can make him helpless. If you do, we will give you five thousand shekels of silver." So Delilah said to Samson, "Tell me, what makes you so strong? What will make you helpless?" Samson replied, "If I were tied up with the strings of seven bows, I would become as weak as an ordinary man." So Delilah tied him up with the strings of seven bows, but Samson snapped them with ease.

JUDGES 16:13–14

Then Delilah said, "You lied to me. Now tell me the truth!" Samson said, "If you weave together seven locks of my hair, I will become as weak as an ordinary man." As Samson slept, Delilah wove together seven locks of Samson's hair. But when he awoke, he pulled his hair free.

JUDGES 16:15–19

Then Delilah said, "How can you say you love me when you don't tell me the truth? Now, what makes you so strong?" Samson had grown tired of her pestering and told her the truth. "I am a Nazirite, devoted to the service of God," Samson said. "If my hair were cut, I would become as weak as an ordinary man." Believing that he had told the truth, Delilah lulled Samson to sleep.

JUDGES 16:18–22

While Samson slept, Delilah cut off all of his hair. His strength slipped away from him. Delilah sent for the Philistines, who seized Samson and gouged out his eyes. They bound him in bronze shackles and threw him into prison, where he became a slave. But Samson's hair began to grow back.

Wind, Breath, and Spirit!

WORD WIZARD

רוּחַ

We first hear the word *ruah* at the beginning of Creation, when a *ruah*—wind—sweeps over the water. We hear it again when the animals board Noah's Ark, two of each kind that have the *ruah*—breath—of life. Now, we hear it again: When Samson needs his great strength, he is gripped by the *ruah*—spirit—of God.

Like wind, breath, and spirit, *ruah* reminds us that God is present—in the air, in our lungs, all around us.

Sculpture of Samson and Delilah from seventeenth-century Belgium

The sin of embarrassing someone, Jewish tradition teaches, may be compared to the sin of murder. In what ways are the two alike?

JUDGES 16:23–25

The Philistines gathered in their temple to offer a sacrifice to their god Dagon. "Our god has given us our enemy Samson," they chanted. They brought Samson from the prison and ordered him to dance for them. Then they tied him up between the two pillars that held the temple up.

JUDGES 16:28–30

Samson called out, "God, please remember me and give me strength just this once, so I may take revenge on the Philistines." Then Samson leaned against two pillars, one with his right arm and one with his left. He cried, "Let me die with the Philistines!" and pushed with all his might. The temple came crashing down. He killed more Philistines in his death than in his lifetime.

In your opinion, was Samson a hero? Why or why not?

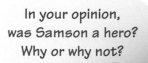

JUDGES 16:31

Samson's family came and took his body to be buried. Samson had led Israel for twenty years.

The Complete Story

Flashback! You are an artist, telling the story of Samson and Delilah. Complete the story by numbering the pictures from 1 to 5 in their correct sequence.

Purpose Puzzle

"You will have a son," God's angel said to Samson's mother. "When he grows up, he will save the Israelites from the Philistines." Though he went on to face many challenges—presented by the Philistines, by Delilah, even by his own people—Samson knew that God had a plan for him: to save the Israelites from the Philistines.

Have you ever felt that you had a special purpose? According to legend, the world is like a giant jigsaw puzzle. Each of us contributes our own, unique puzzle piece to the world. When we do, we help bring shalom, or completeness, to the world.

What do you dream of doing when you grow up? As an adult, how might you use your skills and talents to make the world a more peaceful place? How might you use those abilities now?

A Peace of the Puzzle

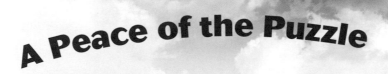

Our sages taught that God makes each person different, one of a kind. No two members of a family or community are the same, no matter how much they have in common. Not even identical twins or best friends are exactly alike. We are all lucky to be different because that's what makes each of us unique and able to enjoy one another and help make the world complete.

Fill in the puzzle pieces of the globe by stating one way in which each person can contribute to making the world more complete and peaceful.

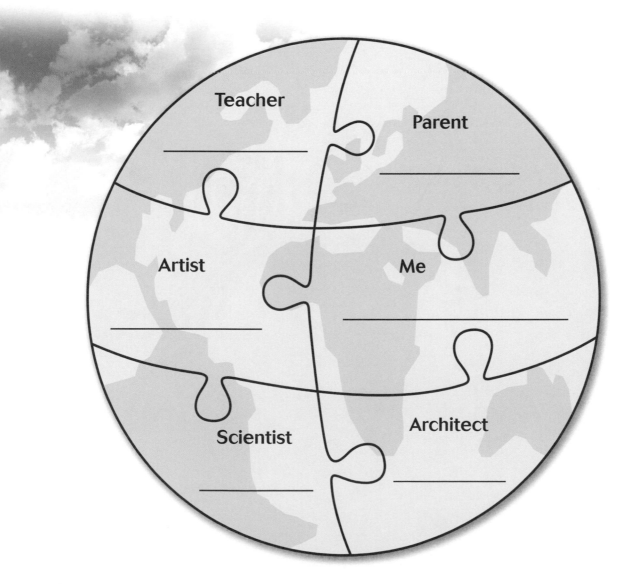

CHAPTER 7

Ruth's Choice

RUTH 1:1–4:17

אל-אשר תלכי אלך

RUTH 1:1–5

There was a famine in the land of Israel. So Naomi, along with her husband Elimelech and their two sons, went to the country of Moab, where food was plentiful. When Elimelech died, Naomi's sons married Moabite women—one named Orpah and the other Ruth. After ten years, Naomi's sons died. Orpah and Ruth were all that was left of Naomi's family.

Because of its lessons of faith and acceptance, we read the Book of Ruth on Shavuot, the holiday on which we celebrate receiving the Torah.

RUTH 1:6–19

Naomi heard that the famine in the land of Israel had ended, and she planned to return to her homeland. Orpah and Ruth wanted to come with her. But Naomi said to them, "Why should you go with me? Stay here, my daughters. Find new husbands and live happy lives. I am too old to marry again, but you are still young. My life is more bitter than yours." Orpah and Ruth began to weep. Orpah kissed Naomi farewell, but Ruth remained with her. "Wherever you go, I will go," said Ruth. "Wherever you stay, I will stay. Your people will be my people, and your God my God." And the two of them traveled together to the land of Israel.

How do you feel when you have to say good-bye to someone you care about?

The Bible teaches that people who are poor may walk behind those who harvest grain, to gather what is left behind.

RUTH 1:22–2:3

Naomi and Ruth arrived in Israel at the beginning of the harvest season. Ruth said to Naomi, "I will go to a field and walk behind the workers as they harvest the grain. Perhaps someone will show me kindness." Naomi replied, "Yes, daughter, go." Ruth went to a nearby field. As luck would have it, the field belonged to Boaz, a wealthy relative of Naomi's husband.

RUTH 2:5–12

When Boaz saw Ruth, he asked his workers, "Who is that girl?" The workers explained who she was and how she came to be there. Boaz said to Ruth, "Stay here, my daughter. Continue to gather food. When you are thirsty, please drink from our water jars." Ruth bowed before Boaz and said, "Why are you being so kind to me? I am not even from this land." Boaz replied, "I have heard what you did for your mother-in-law, how you left your homeland for a people you did not know. May God reward you for what you have done."

Your People Will Be My People

עַמֵּךְ עַמִּי

When someone chooses to become Jewish, that person not only pledges to lead a Jewish life and to perform mitzvot. That person also chooses to become a full member of the Jewish community. Perhaps that is why when Ruth says, "Your people will be my people," we hear the word *am*, "people," twice: *ameich ami*. The Bible is showing us that Ruth is fully aware of her choice to join the Jewish community.

Just as Ruth gathered leftover grain after the harvest, so today the poor of Zimbabwe gather the remains of the field. Our tradition teaches us to remember our ancestor Ruth when we see people in need, and to respond with humility and generosity.

RUTH 2:18–20

When Ruth returned home, she told Naomi of Boaz and his generosity. Naomi said, "Blessed is Adonai, who has shown us great kindness. This man Boaz is one of our relatives!"

Think of three words you would use to describe Boaz.

RUTH 3:1–7

One day, Naomi said to Ruth, "Daughter, I must help you find a home where you will be happy. This is what you should do: Go to Boaz, who is a redeeming kinsman. Dress up in your finest clothing. When Boaz lies down to rest from his work, sneak over to him and lie down near his feet. He will tell you what to do." Ruth did as Naomi had instructed.

At the time of Ruth, it was customary for a close relative—a redeeming kinsman—to marry the wife of a man who had died.

Ruth 3:8–13

In the middle of the night, Boaz awoke with a start—there was a woman lying at his feet! "Who are you?" he asked. Ruth replied, "I am your servant Ruth. I have come to ask you, as a redeeming kinsman, to marry me." Boaz said, "I am moved by your loyalty, especially because you did not seek a younger man, either rich or poor. I wish to do what you ask, for you are an honorable woman. But there is another man who is a closer relative than I am. I must first seek his permission."

Ruth 4:1–11

Boaz met with the man and ten elders of the town. He said to the man, "You are the closest relative, and I am second." The man said, "You may marry the woman. I cannot afford to do so." In Israel at that time, to make a deal official, one man would take off his sandal and hand it to the other. So the man took off his sandal and gave it to Boaz. All the elders said, "May God make the woman Ruth like Rachel and Leah, both of whom built up the House of Israel!"

Ruth 4:13–17

Boaz married Ruth, and they had a son, Obed. Obed was the father of Jesse, who was the father of David, who became king of Israel.

Above and Beyond

MIDRASH MAKER

Question

Why did Boaz ask, "Who is that girl"? What made him notice her and not others gathering grain in his field?

Classic Midrash

When Boaz first saw Ruth, he was impressed by her modesty and respectful manner. While the other women gathered whatever grain they pleased, Ruth obeyed the law and gathered only what had been left behind. While the other women were busy talking with the workers, Ruth was reserved and hardworking. Because of these qualities, Boaz sought to inquire about her. (adapted from Ruth Rabbah 4:6)

Your Midrash

Create your own midrash using this story-starter:

Boaz overheard his workers tell this story of Ruth's kindness: Once, when a fellow worker fell ill and could not gather grain, Ruth _____

_____

_____

_____

_____

_____

_____

_____

Boaz was so impressed by Ruth's actions that he sought to learn more about her.

And He Will Be Nameless

The Bible does not tell us the name of the relative who refuses to marry Ruth. Why? Our sages taught that the man's name is not given because the Bible disapproves of his behavior. Though he gave another excuse, he refused to marry Ruth because she was not born a Jew. But Boaz was rich in both money and learning. He knew that when Ruth converted to Judaism, she became as Jewish as anyone born a Jew.

In the Bible, God tells the Children of Israel, "I make My covenant not only with you, but with all those who are not with us here today." Every Jew who is born and every person who converts to Judaism enters into the covenant between God and the Jewish people.

Each mezuzah case we hang on a doorpost may be unique, but all mezuzah cases contain scrolls with the same words of Torah written on them. In the same way, each Jew may be unique, but all Jews are part of our people's covenant with God.

We've All Got a Share

All Jews—those who are born Jewish and those who choose to become Jewish—share in the Covenant and traditions of the Jewish people. Complete the sentences below to discover some of the many things all Jews are invited to share. Then find those words inside the word search. Words may appear in any direction including backward, diagonally, and upside-down!

1. Deborah was a prophet and a ____ U__ ____ ____ ____.

2. It is a mitzvah to give ____ ____ ____ ____ ____ K__ ____ ____ to those in need.

3. ____ S__ ____ ____ ____ ____ is the homeland of the Jewish people.

4. The Torah teaches us that ____ ____ ____ ____ S__ led the Israelites out of Egypt.

5. On ____ ____ ____ H__ ____ ____ ____ ____ ____ ____ A__ ____ we blow the shofar.

6. The language of the Bible and the Jewish people is __H__ ____ ____ ____ ____ ____.

7. Our tradition teaches that ____ ____ T__ ____ converted to Judaism and was the great-grandmother of King David.

8. We wish each other peace when we say, "____ ____ ____ ____ ____ M__."

```
I  R  R  J  U  D  G  E  A  T  F  F
T  O  L  E  H  R  S  T  S  A  H  O
D  S  D  L  L  E  A  R  S  I  A  O
E  H  E  B  R  O  B  E  Z  T  K  D
E  H  E  B  R  E  W  B  W  G  A  N
P  A  R  U  T  H  T  U  A  M  D  I
Q  S  H  M  B  B  A  T  T  T  E  F
U  H  H  M  O  Y  J  G  D  R  Z  E
I  A  A  X  O  L  I  B  A  L  T  Z
E  N  R  T  R  Y  A  R  T  G  Z  S
T  A  U  Q  I  M  O  H  A  I  L  A
S  H  S  E  S  O  M  B  S  E  Q  P
```

CHAPTER 8

Samuel and the King

1 SAMUEL 1:1–15:11

הֲלוֹא כִּי־מְשָׁחֲךָ יי עַל־נַחֲלָתוֹ לְנָגִיד

1 SAMUEL 1:1–28

In the hill country of Ephraim lived a woman named Hannah. Hannah prayed to God for a child, promising that the child would serve God. God listened to Hannah's prayer, and she gave birth to a son. She named him Samuel, meaning, "I asked God for him." And Hannah prayed:

1 SAMUEL 2:1–10

There is no holy one like God,
Truly, there is none besides You;
There is no rock like our God.

1 SAMUEL 3:1–20

When Samuel was young, his parents brought him to the priest Eli, who became the boy's teacher. One night, God called out to Samuel. Samuel ran to Eli and said, "Here I am." But Eli replied, "I didn't call you. Go back to sleep." God called out to Samuel two more times. Each time Samuel ran to Eli saying, "Here I am." Finally, Eli understood that it was God who called the boy. He said to Samuel, "If God calls you, you must listen." As Samuel grew up, God was with him. During Samuel's lifetime, all of Israel knew that he was a prophet of God.

Describe at least one way in which God may be compared to a rock.

1 Samuel 8:4–9

Later, when Samuel had grown old, the leaders of Israel said to him, "Soon you will die, and we will need someone else to lead us. Give us a king, to rule us like all other nations." Samuel was disappointed in the people—he believed that they should serve only God, not kings. He prayed to God for guidance. God replied, "Listen to what the people have said. But warn them about the practices of any king who may rule over them."

1 Samuel 8:10–22; 9:15–16

Samuel said to the people, "I must warn you: A king will take your sons and make them soldiers in his army. He will take your daughters to be his cooks and servants. He will take your fields and vineyards and give them to his nobles. The day will come when you will cry out because of the king. And God will not answer you on that day." But the people did not listen to Samuel's warning. They said, "We must have a king to rule over us and fight our enemies." And God said to Samuel, "Appoint a king for them." Later, God said to Samuel, "I will send you a man from the tribe of Benjamin, and you will anoint him ruler of My people Israel."

How do you think the people felt at this moment? How did Samuel feel?

1 Samuel 9:1–10

At that time, the tallest and most handsome young man in Israel was Saul, from the tribe of Benjamin. One day, while Saul was tending to his father's donkeys, one of the donkeys went missing. Saul and a servant searched the entire territory of Benjamin but did not find it. Finally, Saul said, "Let us turn back, or my father will worry about us." But the servant replied, "There is a prophet nearby. Perhaps he can help us." Saul replied, "But we do not have gifts to bring him." The servant said, "I have a piece of silver. We will give that to the prophet." And they went to see the prophet Samuel.

1 Samuel 9:19–10:1

When Samuel saw Saul, he said, "I am the prophet you seek. Israel has been waiting for you." When they were alone, Samuel took a flask of oil and poured some on Saul's head. He said, "God anoints you ruler over the people."

In ancient Israel, oil was used to *anoint*, or bless, new kings.

What does Saul's concern for both the stray donkey and his father tell you about his character? If you were in Saul's situation but living in our time, what actions might you take?

Super Saul

MIDRASH MAKER

Question

Why did God choose Saul to be king? What was special about him?

Classic Midrash

God chose Saul because of his humility. After spending much of the day searching for the lost donkey, Saul said to his servant, "Let us turn back, or my father will worry about us." In this way, he made the servant equal to himself. He did not consider the servant less important—to himself or to his father. Then, when Saul sought to avoid becoming king, he ran and hid. Saul was so humble that he did not consider himself worthy of becoming king. (based on Tosefta, Berachot 4:16)

Your Midrash

Go on a Bible scavenger hunt! Read each description of Saul below, then look for a clue in the chapter that proves the description to be true. Write the clues on the lines provided.

Description	Clues
concerned about other people	_____
	_____
modest	_____
	_____
thoughtful and generous	_____
	_____

1 Samuel 10:17–24

Samuel said to the people, "The God of Israel says, 'I brought you out of Egypt and delivered you from slavery. But you have rejected Me by demanding a king. Now I will give you your king—Saul, son of Kish.'" But when they looked for him, Saul was nowhere to be found. They asked where he was and God said, "He is hiding among the baggage." When Saul was brought to him, Samuel said to the people, "This is the one whom God has chosen." And the people shouted, "Long live the king!"

Think of a time when you wanted to hide from responsibility. What were you most concerned about?

1 Samuel 13:1–9

Soon after, the Philistines prepared to attack Israel. Samuel said to Saul, "Gather an army, but wait for seven days, until I return. I will then fulfill God's command to make the customary sacrifices before battle. Only I may do this." But seven days passed, and Samuel did not return. Meanwhile, the Philistine army was camped nearby, with chariots and soldiers as numerous as the sands of the seashore. Saul, afraid to wait any longer, made the customary sacrifices himself. Then he sounded the ram's horn, and the Israelites rallied to help.

1 Samuel 13:10–14:48; 15:10–11

When Samuel arrived, he said to Saul, "What have you done? You disobeyed God's command by making the sacrifices yourself. Now God will seek someone else!" God allowed Saul to defeat the Philistines but said to Samuel, "I regret that I made Saul king. You will now anoint a new king—a ruler after My own heart."

Follow the Crowd?

At the time of Samuel, most of Israel's neighbors were ruled by kings. Kings often treated their citizens harshly, but they provided strong leadership. The tribes of Israel, however, were led by judges such as Deborah and Samson. The judges treated their citizens fairly, but they had limited power. When Samuel grew old, the people of Israel became nervous that their enemies would defeat them. They wanted to do what everyone else did—they wanted a strong leader, a king "like all other nations."

Sometimes it's a good idea to do what everyone else is doing. When everyone is removing their shoes because it's the custom of the home, it's best to follow along. Other times, it's not a good idea. When everyone is making fun of a classmate or throwing food in the cafeteria, it's best to do what is right instead. Like the citizens of Israel, our job is a hard one: to determine when to follow the crowd and when to walk away.

Don't just follow the herd! Judaism teaches that unlike animals, humans have the gift of free will, the ability to choose between right and wrong. Use your free will to decide when to follow the crowd and when to find a better path.

Join in or Walk Away?

Sometimes getting through a school day may feel like making your way through an obstacle course, especially when you must decide whether to follow the crowd or create your own path.

Read the two questions inside each footprint below. Then write two additional questions that can help you decide if the actions you observe others taking are ones you want to join in or walk away from. Be prepared to discuss why your questions would be helpful.

- Are the actions fair?
- Are the actions kind?
- _____
  _____
  _____
- _____
  _____
  _____

- Are the actions safe?
- Are the actions honest?
- _____
  _____
  _____
- _____
  _____
  _____

CHAPTER 9

David's Friends and Foes

1 Samuel 17:1–2 Samuel 5:5

ויקח משה בנו ויקלע

1 SAMUEL 17:1–7

The Philistine army stood on one hill, Saul and his army on another. Both armies were ready for battle. Goliath of Gath, a champion warrior of the Philistines, stepped into the valley between them. Goliath stood six and a half cubits tall. He wore a bronze helmet and a bronze suit of armor and held a bronze spear with an iron head.

A *cubit* is equal to about eighteen inches. That would make Goliath almost ten feet tall!

In the ancient world, nations sometimes settled disputes with individual warriors instead of entire armies.

1 SAMUEL 17:8–32

Goliath called out to Saul's army, "Send one of your men to come down and fight me. If he kills me, we will become your slaves. But if I best him, you will be *our* slaves!" Saul and his army were terror-stricken. David, son of Jesse, a shepherd boy from the tribe of Judah, said, "That Philistine dares to defy the soldiers of God. I will fight him!"

1 SAMUEL 16:21–23; 17:33–37

King Saul was very fond of David. The boy was a skilled harp player whose beautiful music soothed the king when dark moods overcame him. Saul said to David, "You cannot fight him. You are only a boy, and he is a great warrior." David replied, "When a lion or bear would steal one of my father's sheep, I would rescue the sheep from its mouth. If the animal attacked me, I would strike it down and kill it. With God's help, I will do the same to that Philistine." "Then go," Saul replied, "and may God be with you!"

1 SAMUEL 17:40–48

David went down into the valley and approached Goliath. Goliath laughed and said, "Come here. I will give your flesh to the birds of the sky and the beasts of the field." David replied, "You may come against me with sword and spear, but I come against you in the name of God." The Philistine advanced toward David.

This eighth-century BCE sculpture shows a slingshot that may be similar to the one the Bible describes.

God Is With You

יְיָ עִמָּךְ

The words *Adonai im*, "God is with," give us clues to understanding the Bible's message:

● Before David fights Goliath, Saul says to him, "May God be with you."
● Saul becomes jealous of David because "God is with him."
● Jonathan, Saul's son, tells David, "God was once with my father. Now may God be with you."

In this way, the Bible shows us that David will replace Saul and become Israel's new king— and God's chosen leader.

1 SAMUEL 17:49–18:2

David reached into the bag he was carrying, pulled out a stone and a sling, and launched the stone at Goliath. The stone sank into Goliath's forehead and he fell to the ground, dead. David took Goliath's sword and cut off the Philistine's head. The Philistines ran, but Saul's army chased after them and defeated them. That day, Saul made David one of his soldiers.

1 Samuel 18:5–7

David was so successful in battle that Saul made him commander of Israel's army. This pleased the soldiers, because they liked David very much. One day, when the army returned from battle, the women of Israel came out singing and dancing to greet them. Playing timbrels and other musical instruments, they sang:

> Saul has slain his thousands,
> David, his tens of thousands!

1 Samuel 18:8–9

Saul knew that David was successful because God was with him. He also knew that all of Israel loved David. He grew jealous of David's success and popularity—and worried that David might want to become king.

1 Samuel 18:1–3, 20–29

Meanwhile, David became the best friend of Jonathan, Saul's son. They promised to remain loyal to each other forever. Also, at this time, David and Michal, Saul's daughter, fell in love, and the two were married. When Saul realized that both Jonathan and Michal loved David, the king grew still more jealous of him.

Why do you think Saul was jealous of David?

In the Bible, usually a son of the king became the next king. But sometimes God chose someone else. In this case, God chose David.

1 SAMUEL 19:9–20:24

One day while David was playing his harp, a dark mood overcame Saul, and the king threw a spear at David. But David moved out of the way, and the spear got stuck in the wall. David ran to Jonathan and asked, "Why does your father want to kill me?" Jonathan replied, "He won't kill you. My father doesn't do anything without telling me. Go and hide in the field. Meanwhile, I will speak with my father." David did as Jonathan had suggested.

1 SAMUEL 20:28–35

When Jonathan spoke to his father about David, the king flew into a rage. "For as long as David lives, you will never be king. Have David brought to me. He must die!" Jonathan said, "Why? What has he done?" At that, Saul threw his spear at Jonathan. Jonathan ran to find David.

1 SAMUEL 20:41–42

Jonathan went to David's hiding place and said, "Yes, you must flee. God was once with my father. Now may God be with *you*. As for us, we have promised each other to be friends forever. Go in peace!" David and Jonathan embraced each other and wept as they said good-bye.

1 SAMUEL 21:1–2 SAMUEL 5:5

David fled south, to a region called Judah, in the southern part of the Land of Israel. There, he built an army and once again became a strong leader. First, he was made king of Judah. Seven years later, he became king over all of Israel.

The Crowd Goes Wild!

Flashback! **The battle between David and Goliath is about to start.**
Everyone is rooting loudly. Cheer David on by writing some words of support.

Friends Forever

Jonathan and David had one of the most famous friendships in the Bible. Not only did they promise to remain friends—a promise that they kept—but they always helped each other in times of trouble. When Saul wanted to kill David, Jonathan protected his friend. Though Jonathan would have been the next king, he supported David and was not jealous of him. Years later, after Jonathan died, David took care of Jonathan's son.

There are few Jewish values as treasured as friendship. Friendship eases our worries, allows us to see ourselves and the world in exciting, new ways, and makes ordinary things fun. Good friends accept us for who we are and can be happy for us when we win—even if they lose. Because of its unique nature, the rewards of friendship—for you and for your friends—are uniquely precious. As Jonathan and David show us, friendship is a win-win situation.

How do you feel when a friend greets you with a big smile? What do you do to help friends feel valued and respected?

You Light Up My Life

Good friends are precious. Like a rainbow, they can light up a gloomy day or bring a smile to your face. In each color band of the rainbow, write one quality you think is important in a friend. You may choose solely from the qualities below or include other qualities that you think are important.

Be prepared to discuss why you think the qualities are valuable.

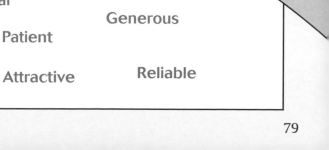

Kind

Trustworthy

Self-confident

Open-minded

Sense of humor

Good listener

Responsible   Popular

Athletic

Generous

Helpful   Fun   Patient

Quiet   Thoughtful of others   Attractive   Reliable

CHAPTER 10

David Stands Guilty

2 SAMUEL 6:1–12:24

אַתָּה הָאִישׁ

2 Samuel 6:1–17

It was a time of great rejoicing. David had conquered the city of Jerusalem and now brought the Ark of God's Covenant up to the holy city. All of Israel rejoiced with shouts and with blasts of the ram's horn. David danced with all his might before God. The Ark of God's Covenant was set in the tent David had prepared for it, and David made sacrifices to God.

To this day, Jerusalem is often called the City of David.

2 Samuel 7:4–29

That night, the word of God came to the prophet Nathan, saying, "Tell David My words: 'I made you ruler of My people Israel. What is more, I will make your name great and protect you from your enemies. After you are gone, your son will be king. He will build a holy Temple for Me, and your family will rule Israel forever.'" When David heard God's words, he said, "Who am I, God, that You have brought me this far? There is none like You and there is no other God but You." David was a fair and just ruler over all of Israel. Because of his leadership, Israel grew into a great kingdom.

When you receive praise, which of these words best describe you: excited, hopeful, humble, or proud? Why *do* you feel that way?

This area of Jerusalem was inside the city walls when the city was under the rule of King David.

2 SAMUEL 11:1–5

One afternoon, while strolling on the roof of his palace, David saw a beautiful woman bathing in a nearby building. David sent a servant to learn more about her. The servant reported, "Her name is Bathsheba. She is the wife of Uriah the Hittite, who is away at battle." David had her brought to the palace. She remained with him awhile, and then returned home. After some time, Bathsheba sent a message to David, saying, "We will soon have a child."

2 SAMUEL 11:6–11

David grew worried about bringing dishonor to himself, so he developed a plan: If Uriah were to go home to his wife Bathsheba, then people would believe that the child is his. So David sent a message to Joab, the commander of his army, saying, "Send Uriah the Hittite to me." When Uriah arrived, David said to him, "Go to your house and rest." But instead, Uriah slept at the entrance of the palace. The next day, David said to Uriah, "Why didn't you go to your house?" Uriah answered, "How can I sleep in my warm, comfortable home when Your Majesty's army is in danger? I cannot do this!"

2 SAMUEL 11:14–27

So David sent a letter to Joab, saying, "Place Uriah where the fighting is fiercest. Then abandon him, so that he is killed." Joab did as David instructed, and Uriah died. Bathsheba mourned for her husband. Later, Bathsheba and David were married, and their son was born. But God was angry with David.

2 SAMUEL 12:1–4

God sent the prophet Nathan to David. Nathan told David this parable:

> There were two men in the same city, one rich and one poor. The rich man had large flocks, but the poor man had only one lamb. The poor man and his family took care of the lamb, and it became like a member of the family to him. One day, a traveler came to the rich man. But instead of taking an animal from his own flocks, the rich man took the poor man's lamb and had it prepared for his guest.

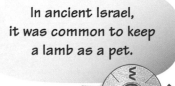

In ancient Israel, it was common to keep a lamb as a pet.

84

Onward and Upward

לְהַעֲלוֹת

The word *l'ha'alot* means "to bring up," but in more than one way. David physically brings the Ark *up* to Jerusalem, a city half a mile above sea level. He also brings the Ark *up* to a higher spiritual place—to Judaism's holiest city.

Today, we hear a form of the word *l'ha'alot* when we have an *aliyah*, the honor of "going up" to the *bimah*. When someone moves to Israel, that person makes *aliyah*, or "goes up" to a higher spiritual place. We hear another form of the word when we describe someone who moves to Israel: an *olah* (female) or an *oleh* (male).

2 SAMUEL 12:5–10

David flew into a rage. He said to Nathan, "That man deserves to die. He will pay for having done such a terrible thing!" Nathan replied, "You are that man! God says to you, 'I anointed you king over Israel and rescued you from the hand of Saul. Why then have you disobeyed My command? Why did you have Uriah killed and then take his wife as your wife? Because you have done this, the sword will never depart from your family.'"

How do you think Nathan felt just before scolding the king? How do you think he felt afterward?

2 SAMUEL 12:13–19

David replied, "I stand guilty before God!" Nathan said, "God will show you forgiveness, because you accept responsibility for having done wrong. However, because of your sin, the child about to be born will die." Soon after, Bathsheba and David's son became ill. David fasted and prayed to God. He refused to be comforted. When the child died, David's servants were afraid to tell him. When David saw his servants talking in whispers, he asked his servants, "Is the child dead?" They replied, "Yes."

2 SAMUEL 12:20–23

David bathed, ate a meal, and prayed. His servants asked him, "Why do you act this way? While the child was alive, you fasted and wept. But now that the child is dead, you return to normal!" David replied, "While the child was alive, I thought, 'Maybe God will have pity on me, and the child will live.' But now, why should I fast? I cannot bring him back."

2 SAMUEL 12:24

Later, David and Bathsheba had another son. Bathsheba named him Solomon.

The Royal Soap Opera

Flashback! **You're a servant in King David's palace. You've overheard some strange conversations these days. Connect each quote to the person who might have said it.**

Nathan

What have I done?
I stand guilty before God!

Bathsheba

How could you have disobeyed God in this way, after all that God has given you?

David

We have tried and tried, but the king refuses to eat. We are worried about him!

David's Servant

Both my husband and my child are dead! Why have such terrible things happened to me?

Who, Me?

It's not easy to accept responsibility. It can mean admitting that we made a mistake, and sometimes having to repair a relationship we've damaged. It can be easier to deny our actions or to blame others. But when we do, we avoid being truthful to those involved—and to ourselves.

When Nathan confronted David, the king could have given excuses for his actions or even had Nathan killed—anything to avoid admitting a mistake. Instead, David chose to be honest with Nathan and with himself. "I stand guilty before God," he said. He accepted responsibility for his actions.

Because we are human, we don't always hit a bull's-eye with our behavior. That's okay. What's important is that we take responsibility for our actions.

No One's Perfect!

Because we're human, we all make mistakes. The good news is that we can learn from our mistakes and try to do better.

Complete the comic strips below to show how someone who has made a mistake can take responsibility and try to do better. You may use drawings or words or both to express your ideas.

CHAPTER 11

Solomon Chooses Wisdom

1 Kings 2:1–8:66

1 Kings 2:1–12

Many years later, as King David lay dying, he said to his son Solomon, "Remember, if you walk in God's ways and keep God's commands, you will succeed in whatever you do." When David died, Solomon became king.

1 Kings 3:5–15

One night, God appeared to Solomon in a dream. "What will I grant you?" asked God. Solomon said, "I am young, with no experience as a leader. Please, grant me an understanding heart and the wisdom to distinguish between good and bad." God was pleased with Solomon's choice. "Because you asked for wisdom instead of a long life or riches," God said, "I will do as you have asked. I will make you more wise than anyone who has ever lived. And I will also give you what you did not ask for—riches and honor your entire life." Then Solomon awoke.

It is believed that David was king around 1000 BCE, more than three thousand years ago.

1 KINGS 3:16–22

Later, two women came before King Solomon. The first said, "Please, my lord! This woman and I live in the same house. I gave birth to a son. Three days later, she also gave birth to a son. During the night, this woman's child died. While I slept, she took my baby from me and replaced him with her dead son. When I arose in the morning, I saw that it was not my baby!" The other woman said, "No, the son that lives is mine, and the dead one is yours!" And they went on arguing, without an end in sight.

1 KINGS 3:24–28

What had King Solomon wisely counted on?

Then Solomon said to his servants, "Bring a sword. Cut the living child in half. Give half to one woman and half to the other." One woman replied, "Please, my lord, give her the live child. Only don't kill it!" The other insisted, "It will be neither yours nor mine. Cut it in two!" The king said, "Give the live child to the woman who asked that it be spared. She is its mother." When the citizens of Israel heard the king's decision, they knew that Solomon was wise indeed.

1 KINGS 5:9–14

In your opinion, what is the difference between wisdom and understanding?

God had given Solomon wisdom and understanding as vast as the sands on the seashore. Solomon composed 3,000 proverbs and 1,005 songs, and was an expert on trees, animals, birds, and fish. People from all nations came to hear his wisdom.

1 Kings 5:16–6:1

One day, Solomon sent this message to King Hiram of Tyre: "I plan to build a temple to honor God. Please, send us cedar wood from Lebanon." When Hiram heard Solomon's message, he was overjoyed. He replied to Solomon, "I will supply all the cedar wood you require. You, in turn, can supply my kingdom with food." In this way, Solomon and Hiram made a treaty. Four hundred and eighty years after the Israelites left Egypt, Solomon began to build the Holy Temple in Jerusalem.

1 Kings 6:2–38

The Temple was built according to Solomon's specific instructions: The walls and floor were made of planks of cypress. Inside was a shrine—the Holy of Holies—in which the Ark of God's Covenant would be kept. Everywhere there were wood carvings of cherubs, palms, and flowers. Bowls, basins, and even the hinges for the doors were made of gold. The entire Temple took Solomon seven years to build.

In biblical times, a cherub was a creature with the face of a human, the wings of an eagle, and the body of a lion. It was a symbol of God's presence.

Holy Ground

MIDRASH MAKER

Question

How did Solomon decide exactly where to build the Holy Temple?

Classic Midrash

King Solomon was unsure where to build the Temple. A heavenly voice called him to Mount Zion, to a field owned by two brothers. One of the brothers was poor, the other blessed with wealth and a large family. In secret, the poor brother added to his brother's heap of grain. After all, his brother had a large family. The rich brother, in the same way, added to the poor brother's heap of grain. After all, his brother was poor. Solomon decided to build the Temple in this field. A place becomes holy, Solomon learned, because of the kindness that takes place there. (a Jewish legend)

Your Midrash

Imagine that Solomon made his decision based on a place *you* consider holy or special. Explain to Solomon why you think the Holy Temple should be built there. Explain what makes it special and how you feel when you are there.

_____

_____

_____

_____

_____

_____

_____

1 KINGS 8:1–66

Then the priests of Israel carried the Ark of God's Covenant into the Temple. In a loud voice, King Solomon blessed the congregation of Israel, "May God be with us. May we walk in God's ways and keep the commandments God gave to our ancestors." And all of Israel was joyful because of the goodness that God had shown them.

This nineteenth-century Shabbat tablecloth shows King Solomon's house and the Temple surrounded by tombs of kings, prophets, and judges.

Good Answer!

If you could ask for anything in the world, what would it be? Your own airplane? An Olympic gold medal? Hot fudge sundaes every day for breakfast, lunch, and dinner?

When God allows Solomon to ask for anything he wishes, the king chooses wisdom. This wisdom allows Solomon to become a respected judge, a gifted writer, and a responsible ruler. Solomon's choice helps him to educate himself and to share his wisdom with others—all without the stomachache. What a wise choice!

A jumbo portion of soda, French fries, and ice cream might make a yummy lunch. But would they be wise choices? What choices might you make that are both yummy and wise?

Wisdom's Way

Travel the path of wisdom by completing the maze below. If you come to a wise decision, you're going the right way. If you come to an unwise choice, you've reached a dead end and must turn back.

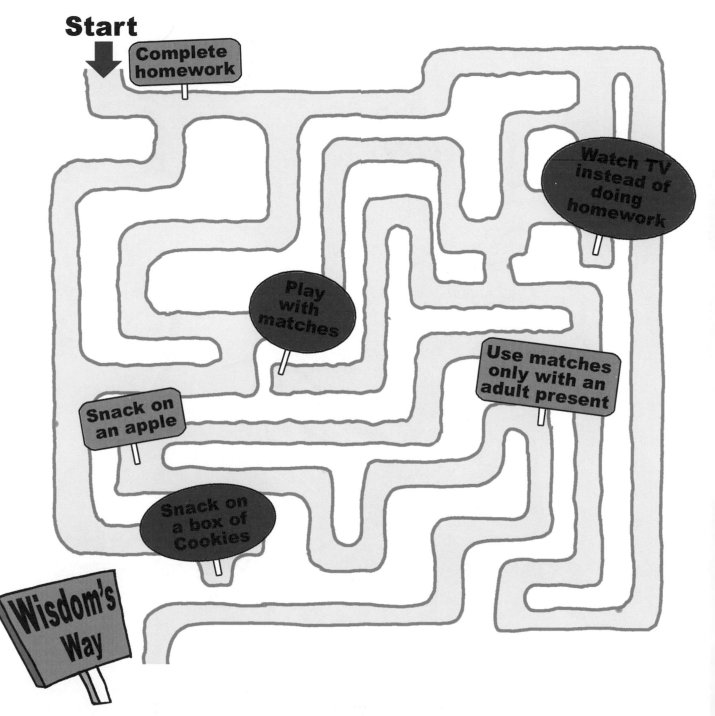

CHAPTER 12

Elijah's Challenge

1 KINGS 12:1–19:21; 2 KINGS 2:1–15

וַיִּמְלֹךְ רְחַבְעָם תַּחַת

1 KINGS 12:1–20

After Solomon died, his son Rehoboam became king. But Rehoboam was not wise like his father. When people in the north complained about the heavy taxes they had paid to Solomon, Rehoboam said, "My father made your burden great, but I will make it greater. My father lashed you with whips, but I will lash you with whips with metal tips." As a result, the Israelites in the north rejected Rehoboam, and the kingdom of Israel split into two: Israel in the north and Judah in the south.

1 KINGS 15:1–16:34

In both Israel and Judah, many kings came and went. Some followed God's commandments; some did not. But none was as terrible as Israel's King Ahab, who worshiped Baal, the god of the Canaanites.

1 KINGS 18:16–20

Elijah the Tishbite, one of Israel's greatest prophets, came before King Ahab. "You have disobeyed God's commandments by worshiping Baal. Now, call all of Israel together, along with the four hundred and fifty prophets who worship Baal, to join me on Mount Carmel." King Ahab did as Elijah had proposed.

The prophet Elijah is said to have performed many miracles, including bringing back to life a child who had died.

Statue of the Canaanite God Baal, from 1300 BCE

1 Kings 18:22–24

Once on Mount Carmel, Elijah announced to the prophets of Baal, "I offer this challenge: You will lay out wood to burn a sacrifice. You will then choose a bull, cut it up, and lay it on the wood—but do not light the fire. I will do the same. You will then call upon your god, and I will call upon my God. The god who responds with fire is the true God." The prophets of Baal accepted Elijah's challenge.

1 Kings 18:26–29

The prophets of Baal called upon their god from morning until noon, shouting, "O Baal, answer us!" But there was no response. They danced around the bull. Still there was no response. When noon came, Elijah mocked them, saying, "Shout louder! He may be on a journey, or perhaps he is asleep." The prophets continued shouting and dancing into the evening, but still there was no response.

Why do you think Elijah mocked the prophets of Baal?

1 Kings 18:36–40

Then it was Elijah's turn. He called out, "God of Abraham, Isaac, and Jacob! Answer me, so that this people may know that You are God." Fire flashed down and took the burnt offering, as well as the wood below it. When the Israelites saw this, they cried out: "The Eternal alone is God!" Then Elijah saw to it that the priests of Baal were punished, according to God's law.

1 Kings 19:16–21

God said to Elijah, "Now you will anoint Elisha son of Shaphat to become prophet after you." Elijah found Elisha plowing in his field. Elijah took off his cloak and wrapped it around Elisha, to show him that he was the new prophet. Then Elisha kissed his father and mother good-bye and followed Elijah. The two men traveled together for several years.

2 KINGS 2:1–8

The time had come when Elijah learned that Elisha knew that God was about to take Elijah to heaven. They stopped at the Jordan River as fifty students of the prophets stood at a distance, watching them. Elijah struck the flowing water with his cloak. The river split in two, so that the two of them crossed over on to dry land.

2 KINGS 2:9–11

As they were crossing the river, Elijah said to Elisha, "Tell me, what can I do for you before I am taken up to heaven?" Elisha answered, "Let your spirit pass on to me." As they were walking, a fiery chariot with fiery horses suddenly appeared, and Elijah went up to heaven in a whirlwind.

What's another example of people crossing through waters that had split in two?

At the close of Shabbat and during the Passover seder, we sing "Eliyahu Hanavi"—Elijah the Prophet—calling upon Elijah to return and bring an age of peace.

WORD WIZARD

The Eternal Alone Is God!

יְיָ הוּא הָאֱלֹהִים

At the end of Yom Kippur, as the sun is about to set, we make the same declaration as did our ancestors on Mount Carmel: *Adonai Hu ha'Elohim*—the Eternal alone is God. As a community we announce, as our ancestors did, that there is one God.

2 KINGS 2:13–15

By the time Elisha reached the opposite bank of the river, the water had again begun to flow. Elisha picked up Elijah's cloak and struck the water. It parted to the right and to the left, and Elisha crossed over. When the students of the prophets saw this, they exclaimed, "The spirit of Elijah has settled on Elisha!" And they bowed low before the new prophet.

All in a Day's Work

TIME TRAVELER

Flashback! **You are Elisha, Israel's new prophet. You have three items on your to-do list and ten hours to complete them. How will you divide your time?**

Write the number of hours you choose to spend on each item.

● Help the king make choices that honor God's laws.

● Challenge and help the Israelites to follow God's laws.

● Pray to God to show kindness to the Israelites.

☐
+ ☐
+ ☐
= 10 Hours

Which item do you consider the most important? Why? _____

_____

_____

_____

Idol Chatter

In the days of Elijah, many Israelites worshiped idols and other false gods. These gods, it was believed, controlled everything—the weather, health, even the future. A good harvest might be a reward from a happy god. A lightning bolt might be a punishment from an angry god—or one in a bad mood. These false gods helped people make sense of the world, but they told people little about what was right and wrong.

Today, we have our own kinds of false gods. We may look to celebrities or fashion to tell us what we want and how to behave. We put our faith in things that we can see and touch. But as Elijah taught us thousands of years ago, we can call out to idols and other false gods from morning until night, but they don't hear us.

At times we may treat our possessions as idols, believing that they can make us better than we are. But they cannot. They are only things. What would it really take to become a better you?

No Faith in the False

Jewish tradition teaches us to put our faith in God, not in false idols. But it can be difficult to put our faith in God because we cannot see or hear God. Sometimes it helps to compare God to people, places, and things that we *can* see and hear.

When we want to say that God is powerful, we may call God a "Ruler." When we want to say that God is caring, we may call God a "Shepherd" and call people "God's flock." Describe God by completing the banner below.

God is _____ like a _____.
(adjective)   (noun)

God's creations—flowers, rivers, rain forests, and people—are like the footprints that are left in the sand by a person we do not see. Each creation reminds us that God is present in the world. Below, draw or describe one of your favorite reminders of God's presence.

CHAPTER 13

Jonah's Message

JONAH 1:1–4:11

JONAH 1:1–3

The word of God came to Jonah, son of Amitai: "Go to the great city of Nineveh and warn its citizens that I have seen their wickedness." But Jonah fled from God's service. He went down to the port city of Jaffa and found a ship going to Tarshish, in the opposite direction of Nineveh. He paid the fare and went down into the ship.

The ancient city of Nineveh lay on the Tigris River, in modern-day Iraq.

JONAH 1:4–6

But God sent a great wind upon the sea, a storm so powerful that the ship was in danger of breaking apart. Terrified, each of the sailors prayed to his own god. They threw the ship's cargo overboard to make it lighter. Meanwhile, Jonah went down into the storage hold of the ship and fell into a deep sleep. The captain of the ship found him and cried out, "How can you sleep? Get up, call upon your god! Perhaps your god will be kind to us, and we will not die."

Jonah went *down* to the port, *down* into the ship, and *down* into the storage hold. What do you think the Bible is telling us about Jonah's situation?

JONAH 1:7–11

The sailors said to one another, "Let us cast lots to find out who is responsible for our misfortune." The lot fell on Jonah. The sailors said to him, "You, who have brought this misfortune, what are you doing here? Who are your people?" Jonah replied, "I am a Hebrew. I worship God, who made both sea and land." Jonah explained that he was fleeing from the service of God. Meanwhile, the storm grew more and more fierce.

When we roll *dice* or draw *straws*, we are *casting lots*—allowing a random outcome to determine what we will do. In ancient times, people believed that by casting lots, they could know the will of God.

107

JONAH 1:11–16

The sailors asked Jonah, "What must we do to calm the sea?" Jonah answered, "Throw me overboard, and the sea will calm down. This storm has come upon you because of me." The men rowed hard to return to the shore, but the storm was growing even worse. Then they cried out to God, "Oh, please, Adonai, do not hold us guilty of killing an innocent person!" They threw Jonah overboard, and the sea stopped raging. The sailors gave thanks to God for causing the storm to stop.

JONAH 2:1–11

Then God sent a giant fish to swallow Jonah. Jonah remained in the belly of the fish for three days and three nights. From the belly of the fish, Jonah prayed to God:

People often say "Jonah and the whale." But the Bible tells us only that it's a *dag gadol*—a giant fish.

> In my trouble I called to God, and God answered me. From the belly of the sea I cried out, and You heard my voice.
>
> You cast me into the heart of the sea, and the floods surrounded me
>
> Yet You brought me up from the pit, Adonai my God!

Then God commanded the fish to spit Jonah out upon dry land.

Archaeologists have discovered objects in Jaffa that are four thousand years old, making it one of the world's oldest port cities. Today, the city of Jaffa is a mixture of modern and ancient sights.

JONAH 3:1–10

The word of God came to Jonah again: "Go to the great city of Nineveh and warn its citizens that I have seen their wickedness." This time, Jonah went at once to Nineveh. He walked through the city, proclaiming, "In forty days, Nineveh will be destroyed!" The people of Nineveh believed Jonah's words. The king of Nineveh told his people, "You must fast, put on sackcloth, and cry out to God. Everyone must turn from their evil ways. Maybe God will forgive us, and we will not die." The people of Nineveh turned from their evil ways, and God did not punish them.

JONAH 4:1–4

This made Jonah very upset. He called out to God, "This is why I fled. I know that You are forgiving and full of kindness, and that you would refuse to punish the Ninevites. So please, take my life, for I would rather die than live." God asked, "Are you that upset?"

Jonah's reaction is very strong. In your opinion, why was he so upset?

A Full Belly

Question

What was it like for Jonah inside the giant fish?

Classic Midrash

The giant fish opened its mouth wide. Jonah entered standing up, as one might enter a big house. The two eyes of the fish were like two windows. A pearl hung from its belly, and like the sun it gave light to Jonah. The pearl made it possible for Jonah to see all around him, in the sea and in the depths. (based on Pirkei d'Rabbi Eliezer 10:47–50)

Your Midrash

Inside the giant fish, write words that describe how Jonah might have felt. For example, he might have felt *grateful* or *lonely*.

Jonah 4:5–9

Jonah left Nineveh and sat down outside the city to see what would happen to it. God provided a plant that grew quickly over Jonah to shade him from the sun. The plant made Jonah very happy. But the next morning God provided a worm that attacked the plant and caused it to wither. The sun beat down on Jonah's head, and he felt faint. He said, "I would rather die than live!"

The Hebrew word for Jonah's plant is *kikayon*. Its translation is a mystery: We don't know what a *kikayon* is. What do you think it might have looked like?

Jonah 4:10–11

Then God said, "You cared about the plant, which you did not work for, which you did not grow, and which appeared and died overnight. Should I not care about the great city of Nineveh, where there are more than a hundred and twenty thousand people who do not know their right hand from their left, as well as many animals?"

Think of one way that you are like Jonah and one way that you are unlike Jonah.

The Biblo-Chat 4000

Time Traveler

Flashback! **You are in the city of Nineveh. You've taken the Biblo-Chat 4000, a computer that sends messages between the past and the present. Help us learn more about Jonah by filling in the blank spaces below.**

Time Traveler: *Why did you run away when God told you to go to Nineveh?*
Jonah:

Time Traveler: *What were you thinking while the storm raged around the ship?*
Jonah:

Time Traveler: *If you could do everything again, what might you do differently?*
Jonah:

A Stormy Story

On Yom Kippur, the Day of Atonement, we make a fresh start. We admit the mistakes we made during the year and promise to do better in the future. We perform *t'shuvah*, which means "returning." We "return" to God in our thoughts and in our actions. Then, as Yom Kippur draws to a close, we read from the Book of Jonah.

Why, on the most holy day of the year, do we read this tale of stormy weather, a giant fish, and a mysterious plant? Because Jonah is a story of *t'shuvah*. Just as the people of Nineveh ask for God's forgiveness, we pray that God will show us compassion and accept our *t'shuvah*.

Don't always feel like accepting someone's apology? Here's a tip: put yourself in the other person's place. It takes courage to apologize for mistakes and to try to do better. Once you think about it, you may find good reasons to be forgiving.

Ship Ahoy!

Complete the crossword puzzle using the clues below.

Across

2. It may take courage to _____ when you've made a mistake.

4. To _____ someone is the opposite of holding a grudge.

6. A worm ate the _____ that had made Jonah happy.

7. God sent a _____ so powerful that it endangered the ship Jonah was on.

8. We pray and fast on _____ _____.

Down

1. God had compassion for the people of _____.

3. _____ was swallowed by a giant fish.

5. *T'shuvah* means that we _____ to God in our thoughts and actions.

6. When we _____, we talk to God.

CHAPTER 14

Isaiah's World of Peace

Isaiah 1:17–32:18

ישַׁעְיָה

The Book of Isaiah is different from the books of the Bible we've studied so far. Instead of a story with characters, it's a collection of the prophet Isaiah's wisdom and teachings—in the form of poetry.

In this chapter, we'll explore Isaiah's vision of a perfect world. What does it look like? How can we get there? Let's go!

ISAIAH 1:16–17

Cease from doing evil
Learn to do good
Dedicate yourselves to justice
Help those who have been wronged
Protect the orphan
Defend the widow

Isaiah lived during a difficult time in Israel's history—a time when its neighbors threatened to destroy it. Isaiah responded by teaching about a perfect world— a world of peace and mitzvot.

ISAIAH 2:4

God will serve as Judge among the nations
They will beat their swords into plowshares
And their spears into pruning hooks
Nation will not lift up sword against nation
And they will study war no more

A *plowshare* is the part of a plow that slices into the earth, allowing seeds to be planted. Why would Isaiah hope that people would "beat their swords into plowshares"?

ISAIAH 11:1–6

A branch will issue from the stump of Jesse
Upon whom the spirit of God will shine
A spirit of wisdom and courage
A spirit of devotion and respect for God
Who will treat the poor with fairness and
    with justice.

At that time
The wolf will dwell with the lamb
The leopard with the young goat

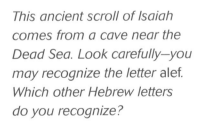

Isaiah predicted the birth of a leader who would bring peace and justice to the world. This leader would be a descendant—or "branch"—of King David, the child of Jesse.

This ancient scroll of Isaiah comes from a cave near the Dead Sea. Look carefully—you may recognize the letter alef. Which other Hebrew letters do you recognize?

Think of a time in your life when being calm and confident helped you to succeed or make a good decision.

ISAIAH 30:15

God said,
 "You will succeed with stillness and quiet
Your victory will come about
Through calm and confidence."

ISAIAH 32:16–18

Then justice will endure in the wilderness
And righteousness will dwell on the field
For the outcome of righteousness will be peace
 with calm and confidence forever
Then my people will dwell in peaceful homes
In safe homes
In untroubled places of rest

Later, the rabbis would echo Isaiah's words in a new way: "The world stands on three things: justice, truth, and peace." (Pirkei Avot 1:18a)

What Lies Ahead?

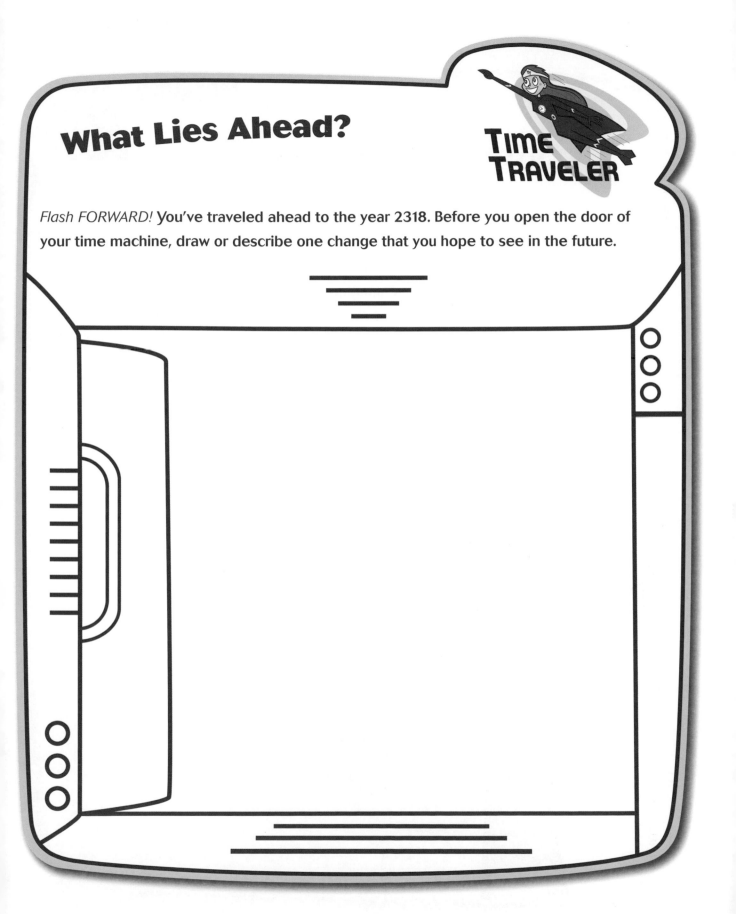

TIME TRAVELER

Flash FORWARD! You've traveled ahead to the year 2318. Before you open the door of your time machine, draw or describe one change that you hope to see in the future.

Making a Difference

Imagine how the world might be if you did an extra mitzvah today. Maybe you can help your sister with her homework or stick up for a classmate. Now imagine doing one extra mitzvah *every day*. Imagine if *everyone* did an extra mitzvah every day. Imagine how the world might be different for you, for those around you, for those yet to be born.

Isaiah imagined a better world, a world of justice and peace, a world without jealousy, hatred, or war. Isaiah helps us to imagine the kind of world that can be possible, if we make it happen. It's up to us.

Sometimes the most important place to perform a mitzvah is at home. How can you express love and respect for your family? How can you add to the peace and kindness in your home?

Chef Shirah Shalom

Chef Shirah Shalom, the singing chef, needs your assistance—pronto! She's cooking her world-famous peace pasta pesto. Y-u-m-m-y! Its secret ingredient is a unique blend of compassion and loving-kindness. That's where you come in. Complete Chef Shirah's recipe by writing, directly in the pasta pot, three caring actions you can take to add peace to your home or classroom.

CHAPTER 15

Jeremiah, the Chosen Prophet

JEREMIAH 1:4–42:12

נחמת ירושלם נתע

JEREMIAH 1:4–8

When Jeremiah was a young boy, the word of God came to him: "Before I created you, I chose you," God said. "Before you were born, I made you holy. I made you a prophet." Jeremiah responded, "But Eternal One, I do not know how to speak—I am still a boy." God said, "Go where I send you, and speak what I command you. Have no fear, for I am with you."

Like Moses, Jeremiah tells God that he is not worthy of his mission. Think of a time when *you* thought at first you couldn't succeed—and then did.

JEREMIAH 26:1–6

Years later, when Jeremiah was a man, the word of God came to him again: "The priests and prophets of the Temple have done what is wrong in My sight. They care only about making sacrifices in the Temple, not about living by My Torah that I gave them. Now, stand in the courtyard of the Holy Temple in Jerusalem. Tell the people there that if they change their ways, I will not punish them." Jeremiah did as God had commanded.

JEREMIAH 26:11–16

When the priests and prophets of the Temple heard Jeremiah's words, they shouted, "This man should die for saying such things!" But the people said, "This man should not die, for he brings us the word of God. He wants only to protect us."

JEREMIAH 32:26–35

More than twenty years passed. God gave Jeremiah two messages, one of tragedy and one of hope. They began: "The people of Israel and Judah have done nothing but evil in My sight. They turned their backs on My Teaching and worshiped idols. Because of this, I am giving Jerusalem to the Babylonians, who will set the city on fire and burn it down. They will exile the people to a faraway land."

By My Torah

בְּתוֹרָתִי

When God reminds us to live *b'torati*, "by My Torah," we may think of the scroll we read in synagogue. But the closer we look at the word *Torah*, the more we discover.

Torah is related to the Hebrew word meaning "to shoot," the word we use when shooting an arrow. It's also related to the word *morim*, meaning "teachers." What do these words have in common? *Guidance*. Just as we guide an arrow in the right direction, as our teachers guide us, the Torah guides us in the right direction. Jeremiah knew that without Torah's guidance, it's easy to become lost.

JEREMIAH 32:36–40

But then God continued, "However, I will then gather the people from the land of exile, and I will bring them back to this place. They will be My people, I will be their God, and I will make with them an everlasting covenant.

Jewish tradition teaches us that God shows us a balance of din, or judgment, and raḥamim, or mercy.

JEREMIAH 36:1–10

The word of God came to Jeremiah another time: "Get a scroll and record the words I have spoken to you." So Jeremiah called the scribe Baruch, who wrote the words of God while Jeremiah spoke them aloud. Then Jeremiah said, "I cannot go to the Temple. Because I warned the people to change their ways, I am hiding from the king in fear. But you go and read the words of God to the people." Baruch did as Jeremiah instructed him.

JEREMIAH 36:11–32

When the people heard the words that Baruch spoke, they became afraid. The scroll was taken from Baruch and delivered to the king. The king sat by a blazing fire and listened as a servant read the words aloud. As he listened, the king sliced off sections of the scroll and threw them into the fire. He did this until the entire scroll was burned. But God instructed Jeremiah to get another scroll and record the same words that were in the first. So once again Baruch wrote the words of God while Jeremiah spoke them aloud.

Think of a way in which writing has been important to the Jewish people. Think of a way in which writing has been important to you.

JEREMIAH 38:17–39:8

Later, Jeremiah gave the same warning to Zedekiah, the new king of Judah. If he did not offer peace to the Babylonians, Jeremiah warned, Jerusalem would be burned down. But the king refused to surrender. Then, just as Jeremiah had predicted, the Babylonian army entered Jerusalem and conquered it. They tore down the walls of Jerusalem and burned down King Zedekiah's palace. They forced the king to watch as they killed his sons. Then they put out the king's eyes and sent him to prison for the rest of his life. Many people were taken from their homes and sent into exile in Babylonia.

JEREMIAH 42:1–12

The Jews who remained in Jerusalem said to Jeremiah, "There are only a few of us left here. Let God tell us where we should go and what we should do." Jeremiah replied, "God says to you, 'If you remain here, I will rebuild your community. Do not be afraid of the king of Babylonia, for I will rescue you from his hands. I will see that he is merciful to you. I will see that your land is restored to you.'"

The Jews who were exiled to Babylonia faced a great challenge: surviving without a Temple or a homeland.

Jeremiah told the Jews who were exiled to Babylonia, "Build houses and live in them. Plant gardens and eat their fruits....Multiply there, do not decrease in numbers." (Jeremiah 29: 5–6) Why was this wise advice?

What Now?

Flashback! **You've been exiled from Jerusalem to faraway Babylonia. Make a list of ways in which you can live a Jewish life and help the Jewish community remain strong, even though you are far from home.**

Kid Power

When Jeremiah was a boy, God told him that he had been made a prophet. Why would God give such an important job to someone so young? One answer may be found in this midrash:

When the Israelites stood at Sinai, God said, "I am prepared to give you my Torah, My prized possession. In return, you must give me a guarantor—someone who will take care of My Torah." Israel said, "Our ancestors are our guarantor." God said, "Your ancestors are not suitable as a guarantor." Israel said, "The prophets are our guarantor." God said, "The prophets too are not suitable as a guarantor." Israel said, "Dear God, our children are our guarantor." And God said, "Your children are a good guarantor. It is for their sake that I give the Torah to you." (adapted from Shir Hashirim Rabbah 1:4)

This midrash, like the Book of Jeremiah, reminds us that young people—like you—represent the future of the Jewish people. Because of this, you are valuable beyond measure.

V'ahavta, one of Judaism's most important prayers, reminds us to teach God's words to our children. Even the youngest child who performs a mitzvah contributes to the future of our people and tradition.

It's a Mitzvah!

The Torah is so precious to the Jewish people that it is often called the Tree of Life. When you follow the Torah's teachings by performing a mitzvah it is like tasting the fruit of the Tree of Life. In addition, each mitzvah you perform adds life to our people and promise to our future.

Read the list below. Then write each item that is a mitzvah on one fruit of the Tree of Life. There is an extra fruit on which you can write an additional mitzvah.

- Call a foul

- See a movie

- Study Torah

- Shake a leg

- Help a parent

- Feed a pet

- Give tzedakah

- Call a sick friend

- Shake a *lulav* and *etrog*

- Light Shabbat candles

- Help yourself to cake

CHAPTER 16

Queen Esther Saves the Jews

ESTHER 1:1–9:26

וַתֹּאמֶר אֶסְתֵּר אִישׁ צַר וְאוֹיֵב הָמָן הָרָע הַזֶּה

ESTHER 1:1–15

Long ago, in the Persian city of Shushan, King Ahasuerus threw a banquet for all of his officials and noblemen. As the banquet was drawing to a close, the king ordered his queen, Vashti, to show off her beauty before his guests. But Queen Vashti refused to obey the king's command. The king burned with fury. He asked his advisers what he should do.

ESTHER 1:16–21

The king's advisers replied, "You must find a new queen. If not, marriages throughout the kingdom will fall apart. Let the beautiful young women of the kingdom be brought to the palace. The one whom Your Majesty chooses will become the new queen." The idea pleased the king.

The Book of Esther tells the story of one of our most joyful celebrations: Purim.

ESTHER 2:1–20

Soon, many contestants arrived at the king's palace, hoping to become the new queen. Among them was a beautiful Jewish woman named Esther. Esther was a younger cousin of a Jew named Mordechai, who had adopted her when her parents died. Mordechai had told Esther not to reveal that she was Jewish. When King Ahasuerus saw Esther, he loved her more than all the other women. He placed a royal tiara on her head and made her queen. He treated her with special kindness. Still, Esther did not reveal that she was a Jew.

ESTHER 2:21–23

One day, Mordechai overheard a conversation between two of the king's guards. They were plotting to kill King Ahasuerus! Mordechai told this to Queen Esther, who repeated Mordechai's words to the king. The two guards were found guilty and were hanged on the gallows. This was recorded in the royal book of records.

ESTHER 3:1–13

Later, King Ahasuerus appointed a man named Haman to be his highest official. The king ordered all citizens to bow before Haman. But Mordechai would not bow, for he was a Jew. Haman, filled with rage, decided to destroy all the Jews. Haman said to the king, "These people do not obey Your Majesty's laws. Please, issue a ruling that they should be destroyed." The king agreed, so Haman cast *purim*, "lots," to determine on which day the Jews should be killed. It was decided that the Jews would be killed on the thirteenth day of the twelfth month, the month of Adar.

For the first time in the Bible, a person is referred to as a *Jew*. Before that, we were called Hebrews, Israelites, or Children of Israel.

Why do you think that Haman wanted to kill *all* Jews? Why not only Mordechai?

Esther Calls It a Day

MIDRASH MAKER

Question

How did Esther maintain her Jewish identity in a non-Jewish world?

Classic Midrash

In the king's palace, Esther had almost no contact with other Jews. In fact, she was in danger of forgetting when Shabbat had come. So she gave her seven servants names that would help her mark the passage of time. On Tuesday, for example, she was served by Genunita, meaning "garden," for on the third day plants were created. On Friday she was served by Hurfita, "little lamb," for on the sixth day animals came into being. On Shabbat, she was served by Rego'ita, meaning "rest." In this way she remembered the day of Shabbat week after week. (based on Targum Esther 2:9)

Your Midrash

Tell about a time when you felt like you were in the minority as a Jewish person. What helped you remember that you were Jewish? In what ways were you proud to be a Jew?

_____

_____

_____

_____

_____

_____

_____

This Scroll of Esther was made in Italy. We read the Megillah on Purim. What other customs do we observe on Purim?

ESTHER 4:1–5:5

Jews throughout the kingdom mourned and wept upon hearing the king's ruling. Mordechai said to Esther, "You must speak to the king, even though you put your life in danger by approaching him without being summoned. Who knows—perhaps you have become queen to save the Jews." Esther put on royal clothing and came before the king. "What is your request, Queen Esther?" the king asked her. "If it please Your Majesty," Esther said, "come to a feast that I have prepared in honor of Your Majesty and Haman." The king accepted Esther's invitation.

ESTHER 6:1–4

That night, the king could not sleep. He called his servants and ordered them to read aloud from the royal book of records. As his servants read, the king was reminded of what Mordechai had done to save his life. He asked, "How have we honored Mordechai the Jew for this?" His servants replied, "Nothing at all has been done for him." At that moment, Haman entered the royal palace, seeking permission to have Mordechai hanged on the gallows that he had already set up.

ESTHER 6:6–10

The king asked Haman, "What should be done for a man the king wishes to honor?" Haman said to himself, "The king must want to honor me!" So he replied, "This man should be dressed in royal clothing, with a royal crown on his head. He should be paraded on a horse through the city, while people praise his name." "Yes!" said the king. "Get the clothing and the horse, as you have said, and do this for Mordechai the Jew."

Imagine the look on Haman's face at this moment!

ESTHER 7:1–8:14

It was the day of the banquet that Queen Esther had prepared for the king and Haman. So that both men could hear her, Esther said, "Please, Your Majesty, spare my life and the lives of my people. Someone has seen to it that we are to be destroyed!" The king demanded, "Who dares to do this?" Esther replied, "The foe and enemy is the evil Haman!" The king was furious. He had Haman hanged on the gallows that had been set up for Mordechai. The king issued a ruling that the Jewish people may defend themselves against anyone who might attack them. In this way, the Jews avoided disaster.

ESTHER 8:15–9:26

Everywhere, the Jews celebrated. Cries of joy were heard throughout the city of Shushan. The fourteenth day of Adar, the day after which the Jews were to be killed, was made a holiday of feasting and gladness—and an occasion for sending gifts to one another. Because Haman had chosen the day by casting *purim*, "lots," the holiday was named *Purim*.

The Book of Esther does not mention God. Why do you think that is? (There is no right answer!)

Happiness and Joy

שִׂמְחָה

Today, a special occasion such as a bat mitzvah or a wedding is called a *simḥah*—a time of happiness and joy. For the Jews of Shushan, the fourteenth of Adar was an especially sweet *simḥah*—a day to celebrate Queen Esther's courage in saving the Jews. In fact, the Bible uses the word *simḥah* seven times to describe how joyful a day it was!

The *simḥah* for the Jews of Shushan is a lot like a *simḥah* today—they are both reasons for the entire Jewish community to celebrate.

All for One

Our sages taught us that *kol yisrael areivim zeh bazeh*—all Jews are responsible for one another. Queen Esther lived by this lesson. She risked her life to save her fellow Jews when they needed her help.

Today, there are Jewish communities around the world that need our help. In some places, Jews are not allowed to practice their religion openly. In many countries— even in North America—there are Jews who do not have enough money to buy food. Just as Queen Esther did so many years ago, we must remember the lesson of *kol yisrael areivim zeh bazeh*. **Being part of the Jewish community is like being a member of one big family.**

Marching in an Israel Day Parade is one way to show your support and concern for other Jews.

Caring Connections

Use the questions below to help you think of ways to reach out and create caring connections between yourself and other members of the Jewish community, as well as with Jews around the world.

1. How can you help Jews in need of food and clothing?
2. What can you contribute to making your religious school a friendly place?
3. Whom might you contact to help Jews who are oppressed?
4. What can you do to strengthen your connection with Israel?
5. How can you help welcome new members of your synagogue?
6. How can you help a religious school classmate who is ill?

CHAPTER 17

Daniel's Risk

DANIEL 1:1–6:28

DANIEL 1:1–2:48

It was a difficult time for the Israelites. King Nebuchadnezzar of Babylonia had taken many of them from their homes and sent them to Babylonia. There, he established a school to train young Israelite men to spend their lives serving him. One student, Daniel, impressed the king with his wisdom. The king appointed Daniel governor of Babylonia and chief of all his wise men.

DANIEL 3:1–20

Sometime later, King Nebuchadnezzar made a statue of gold. "Whoever does not bow down to the statue," it was proclaimed, "will be thrown into a burning fiery furnace." Three of Daniel's fellow Jews—Shadrach, Meshach, and Abednego—would not bow down. Those who hated the Jews took advantage of this. They told the king, "There are three Jews who do not worship the statue of gold." The king, in a fury, gave an order to heat up the furnace to seven times its usual heat. He gave an order that Shadrach, Meshach, and Abednego be thrown into the furnace.

What other people in the Bible were famous for their wisdom?

*Babylonian ruins
from the time of
King Nebuchadnezzar*

Daniel 3:21–33

King Nebuchadnezzar watched as Shadrach, Meshach, and Abednego were dropped, bound by ropes, into the furnace. Suddenly, he exclaimed, "I see men walking about in the fire!" Then the three men walked out of the furnace. The fire had no effect on them—not even the hair on their heads had been burnt. Nebuchadnezzar said, "I hereby give an order that anyone who speaks against the God of Shadrach, Meshach, and Abednego will be torn limb from limb!" And the king gave thanks to God.

DANIEL 5:1–11

Later, Nebuchadnezzar's son Belshazzar became king of Babylonia. One evening, Belshazzar and his officials sat drinking wine from vessels that were stolen from the Holy Temple in Jerusalem, giving praise to gods of gold. Suddenly, the fingers of a human hand appeared on the palace wall and began to write. The king was terrified. He called, "Whoever can read this writing will receive great riches and power!" The king's wise men arrived, but they could not read the writing. The queen said, "O King, there is a man in your kingdom who has wisdom like that of the gods. Your father once appointed him chief of the wise men."

The expression "see the writing on the wall," used when we suspect that bad things will happen, comes from this story.

DANIEL 5:13–29

Daniel was brought before the king. He said, "Your Majesty, your father was powerful. When he grew arrogant and vain, however, he was taken from his throne. And you, though you know this, do not humble yourself. You praise gods of gold, which do not see, hear, or understand. Therefore, God caused the hand to appear. The writing is a warning that your kingdom will soon be given to your enemies." Belshazzar was so impressed by Daniel's ability that he made Daniel a great ruler in his kingdom.

DANIEL 6:1–10

Later, Daniel served as an officer for another king, King Darius. Because of Daniel's excellent spirit, Darius considered making him the highest official in the kingdom. The other officers became jealous of Daniel and looked for ways to turn the king against him. They said to King Darius, "We recommend that you issue a ruling: Whoever worships any god or man

What do you think it means to have "excellent spirit"? Who do you know who has "excellent spirit"?

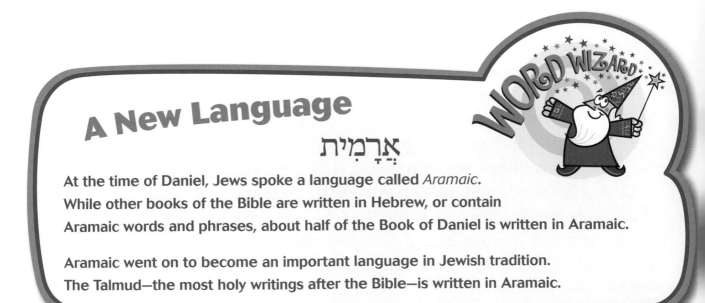

A New Language

אֲרָמִית

WORD WIZARD

At the time of Daniel, Jews spoke a language called *Aramaic*.
While other books of the Bible are written in Hebrew, or contain
Aramaic words and phrases, about half of the Book of Daniel is written in Aramaic.

Aramaic went on to become an important language in Jewish tradition.
The Talmud—the most holy writings after the Bible—is written in Aramaic.

besides you, O King, will be thrown into a lions' den."
The king agreed, and the ruling was issued.

DANIEL 6:11–18

When Daniel heard about the ruling, he became worried. He went to his house, stood facing Jerusalem, and prayed to God. At that moment, the officers of the king entered his house and saw Daniel in prayer. They said to the king, "Daniel has disobeyed the ruling, O King. You must throw him into the lions' den." The king, who was fond of Daniel, wanted to save him. But he knew that the ruling could not be changed. So Daniel was thrown into the lions' den. To prevent him from escaping, a rock was placed over the entrance to the den.

For centuries, Jews have faced Jerusalem as we pray. Why do you think that is?

DANIEL 6:20–25

At dawn, the king rushed to the lions' den. He cried, "Daniel, was your God able to save you from the lions?" Daniel replied, "My God sent an angel who found me innocent. He shut the mouths of the lions, so that they did not injure me." Daniel was brought up out of the den, and the officers who spoke against Daniel were thrown in. The lions quickly overpowered the officers and crushed their bones.

DANIEL 6:26–28

Then King Darius wrote to all peoples of the earth, "I hereby give an order that all must respect the God of Daniel, who performs signs and wonders in heaven and on earth—for God has saved Daniel from the power of the lions!"

The Duke of Rebuke

Daniel scolded Belshazzar for turning from God and worshiping idols. By doing this, he put himself at risk. But instead of saying nothing or being dishonest, Daniel *rebukes* Belshazzar. He tells the ruler that what he had done is wrong.

Judaism teaches us to let others know when they have done something wrong. That includes speaking up when classmates are hurtful to others, like when they gossip or play too rough on the soccer field. Or when friends are hurtful to themselves, like when they ride a bike without a helmet or don't study for tests. This rebuke is called *tocheiḥah*. Like Daniel, our challenge is not only to speak up but also to do so in a way that is both respectful and appropriate.

When we privately and respectfully rebuke someone for behaving inappropriately, tocheiḥah *can be an act of kindness. But when we rebuke someone in public or with harsh words, we ourselves become guilty of poor behavior.*

A Little Sensitivity, Please!

While it may be important to let others know when they have done something wrong, it is equally important to do so in a respectful and caring way. We must use the right words and the right tone of voice, and find the right time and place when rebuking somone. It can make the difference between scolding someone and helping the person understand how to act in a better way.

In each column, put a check (✓) next to the words, tone, or place you consider most appropriate when rebuking someone.

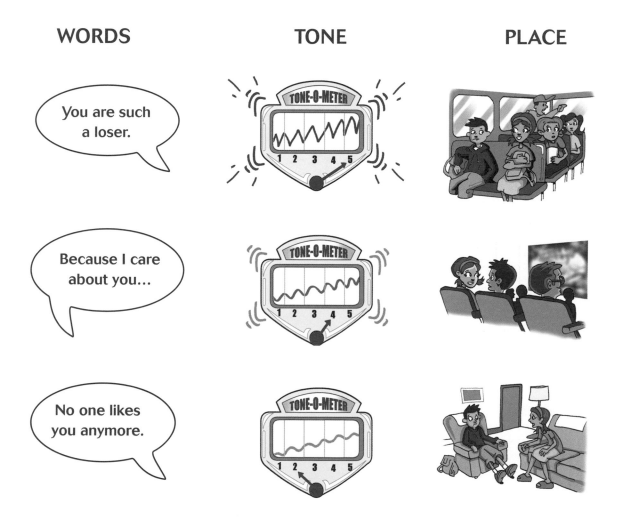

WORDS   **TONE**   **PLACE**

A tip from Jewish tradition: **Judaism teaches that before we rebuke someone, we must look at our own behavior. We must ask ourselves whether we have committed the same wrongdoing. If we have, we must first correct our own behavior.**

CHAPTER 18

Ezra and Nehemiah Rebuild Jerusalem

EZRA 1:1–6:18; NEHEMIAH 1:1–8:9

וַיִּפְתַּח עֶזְרָא הַסֵּפֶר לְעֵינֵי כׇל־הָעָם

EZRA 1:1–65

King Cyrus of Persia had defeated the Babylonians and now ruled the Land of Israel. God stirred the spirit of the king, who sent a proclamation throughout his kingdom. "God has ordered me to rebuild the Holy Temple in Jerusalem," Cyrus said. "All of God's people may return to their homeland and begin to build." Cyrus then returned the gold and silver bowls and vessels that had been taken from the Temple, and fifty thousand Jews left Babylonia to rebuild the Holy Temple.

EZRA 3:10–13

When the builders finished the foundation of the Temple, they sang, "God's love for Israel is eternal!" The elders of the community—those who remembered the First Temple—wept loudly at the sight. Others shouted joyously at the top of their voices, the sound of which could be heard from afar.

Unlike the Babylonians, who ruled before them, the Persians were tolerant of the Jews and allowed them to worship freely.

149

Think of a goal that you reached after a great deal of time and effort. How did it feel?

EZRA 4:1–6:18

But the enemies of the Jews tried to make the builders afraid to build. They even lied to King Cyrus, saying that the Jews wanted to rise up against him. Sometimes Cyrus allowed the builders to continue, other times not. The progress was slow. But after more than twenty years, the Temple was finally finished. The people celebrated and made sacrifices to God. But the enemies of the Jews continued to harass them.

Horn-shaped drinking cup from the time of King Cyrus

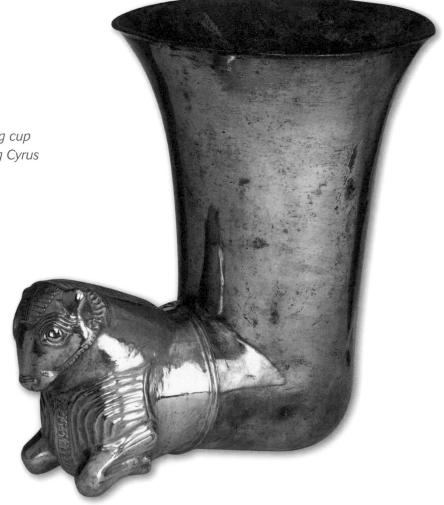

NEHEMIAH 1:1–2:9

About a hundred years later, the Jews were once again threatened by their enemies, who had damaged the walls of Jerusalem. A Jew named Nehemiah, who was a high-ranking official in the Persian court, was deeply upset by this news. He said to the king, "Your Majesty, the city of my ancestors is in dire condition, and its gates have been consumed by fire." The king said, "What is your request?" "If it please the king," Nehemiah responded, "send me to Jerusalem to help rebuild it." The king agreed, and Nehemiah went to Jerusalem.

Nehemiah's name means "God is my comfort."

NEHEMIAH 2:11–18

During the night, Nehemiah, along with a few men, secretly inspected the damaged walls and gates of the city. Nehemiah said to the men, "You see the bad state we are in—Jerusalem lying in ruins. Come, let us rebuild the wall!" The men were inspired by Nehemiah and said, "Let us start building!"

NEHEMIAH 3:1–4:7

The building went quickly because the people's heart was in the work. But again the enemies of the Jews came together, and said to themselves, "Before they know it, we will attack and kill them. We will put a stop to the work." But the Jews prayed to God and set up guards along the walls, to keep lookout during the day and at night.

NEHEMIAH 4:8–4:17

Some people worked, while some held swords and shields. Others worked with one hand while holding a weapon in the other. "Do not be afraid of our enemies," Nehemiah told them. "Think of what God has done for you, and fight for your homes, your brothers, and your sons and daughters!" In this way the people repaired and defended the walls of Jerusalem.

NEHEMIAH 8:1–6

To this day, we rise when the Torah is removed from the Ark. Why do you think we do this?

Ezra the Scribe, who had also earlier arrived from Babylonia, was an expert in the Teaching of Moses. On Rosh Hashanah, he assembled the people at the Water Gate in Jerusalem and brought the Torah before the congregation. He opened the scroll for all the people to see, and all the people stood up. Ezra blessed God's name, and the people answered, "Amen, Amen."

NEHEMIAH 8:7–9

Why do you think the people wept upon hearing the Torah read?

Ezra then read from the scroll of the Torah. He explained the meaning of the words so that everyone would understand. The people wept as they heard the words of the Torah.

Something to Write Home About

MIDRASH MAKER

Question
Why was Ezra called Ezra the *Scribe*?

Classic Midrash
Before Ezra died, he collected all the holy writings and brought them together in one place. He called upon God to help him record all that had happened since the creation of the world. God instructed Ezra to select five scribes and to dictate to them for forty days. After one day, a voice called to Ezra, "Open your mouth, and drink what I give you." Ezra opened his mouth and received a drink that flowed like water but was the color of fire. This drink sustained him for forty days as he dictated to the scribes. (adapted from 4 Ezra 3–14)

Your Midrash
Imagine that you are creating a "family bible" to record the story and history of your grandparents, your parents, and yourself. What would you include in your bible? How would you gather information?

Three people I would interview:

_____   _____   _____

Three stories I would be sure to include:

1. _____

2. _____

3. _____

In your opinion, why is it important not only to tell these stories, but also to write them down?

_____

_____

The Courage to Start Again

Think of a time in your life when you rebuilt something that had been lost or destroyed. How did it feel, knowing that so much work and time had gone to waste? It can be hard to rebuild and to start again. It takes courage and determination.

Ezra and Nehemiah understood this. Nehemiah understood that it would take a great effort—by himself and by those around him—to rebuild the walls of Jerusalem. Ezra understood that it would require dedication to rebuild the spirit of the Jews by teaching Torah. Ezra and Nehemiah taught us that rebuilding can be hard—perhaps one of the greatest challenges of our lives—but the rewards are even greater: a strong, growing, and confident community.

No matter how great the task, we can meet any challenge if we each offer a helping hand.

Quality Building Blocks

Courage and determination often are required to rebuild something that has been lost or destroyed. Select six qualities from the list below that can help the process of rebuilding. Write one quality in each building block. Add two building blocks and label each with an additional quality that you think could be valuable.

Be prepared to discuss the value that each quality you have selected can add to the process of rebuilding.

- Patience
- Sense of humor
- Flexibility
- Maturity
- Practicality
- Self-confidence
- Reliability
- Discipline
- Persistence

Timeline

Timeline

Israelites leave Egypt and receive Ten Commandments

Joshua leads Israelites into Canaan

Deborah

Samson

Ruth and Noami

1300 BCE

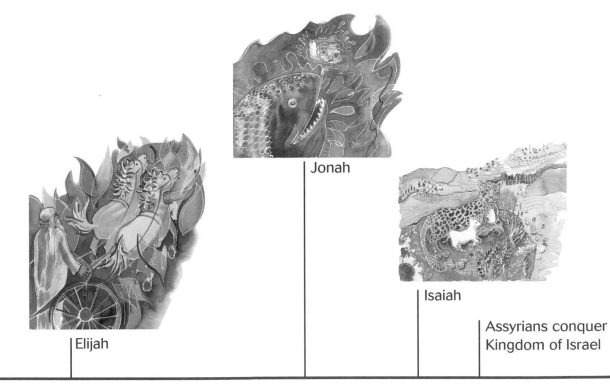

Elijah

Jonah

Isaiah

Assyrians conquer Kingdom of Israel

900 BCE

King Saul

King David

King Solomon

Solomon builds
Holy Temple

900 BCE

Jeremiah

Babylonians
conquer
Kingdom
of Judah;
First Temple
destroyed

Daniel

Temple rebuilt

Ezra and
Nehemiah

Esther

400 BCE